MW00559393

For Hector, who likes maps.
With love, E.H.

To my favorite little explorers, Laurice and Alonzo, for being a constant source of joy and energy while making this book. L.B.

Brimming with creative inspiration, how-to projects and useful information to enrich your everyday life, Quarto is a favorite destination for those pursuing their interests and passions.

First published in 2022 by Wide Eyed Editions, an imprint of The Quarto Group.
100 Cummings Center, Suite 265D, Beverly, MA 01915, USA.
T +1 978-282-9590 F +1 078-283-2742 www.Quarto.com

A CIP record for this book is available from the Library of Congress.

ISBN 978-0-7112-6282-9

The illustrations were created digitally.
Set in Bruce Standard and Quicksand

Published by Georgia Amson-Bradshaw
Designed by Myrto Dimitrakoulia
Commissioned by Lucy Brownridge
Edited by Alex Hithersay and Lucy Brownridge
Production by Dawn Cameron

Manufactured in Guangdong, China CC052022

9 8 7 6 5 4 3 2 1

Written by Emily Hawkins

Illustrated by Lauren Baldo

An Atlas of Lost Kingdoms

Discover Mythical Lands, Lost Cities and Vanished Islands

WIDE EYED EDITIONS

Arctic Ocean
North America
Europe
Atlantic Ocean
Afric
Central America
Pacific Ocean
South America
World Map

ASIA
INDIAN
OCEAN
AUSTRALASIA
SOUTHERN
OCEAN

CONTENTS

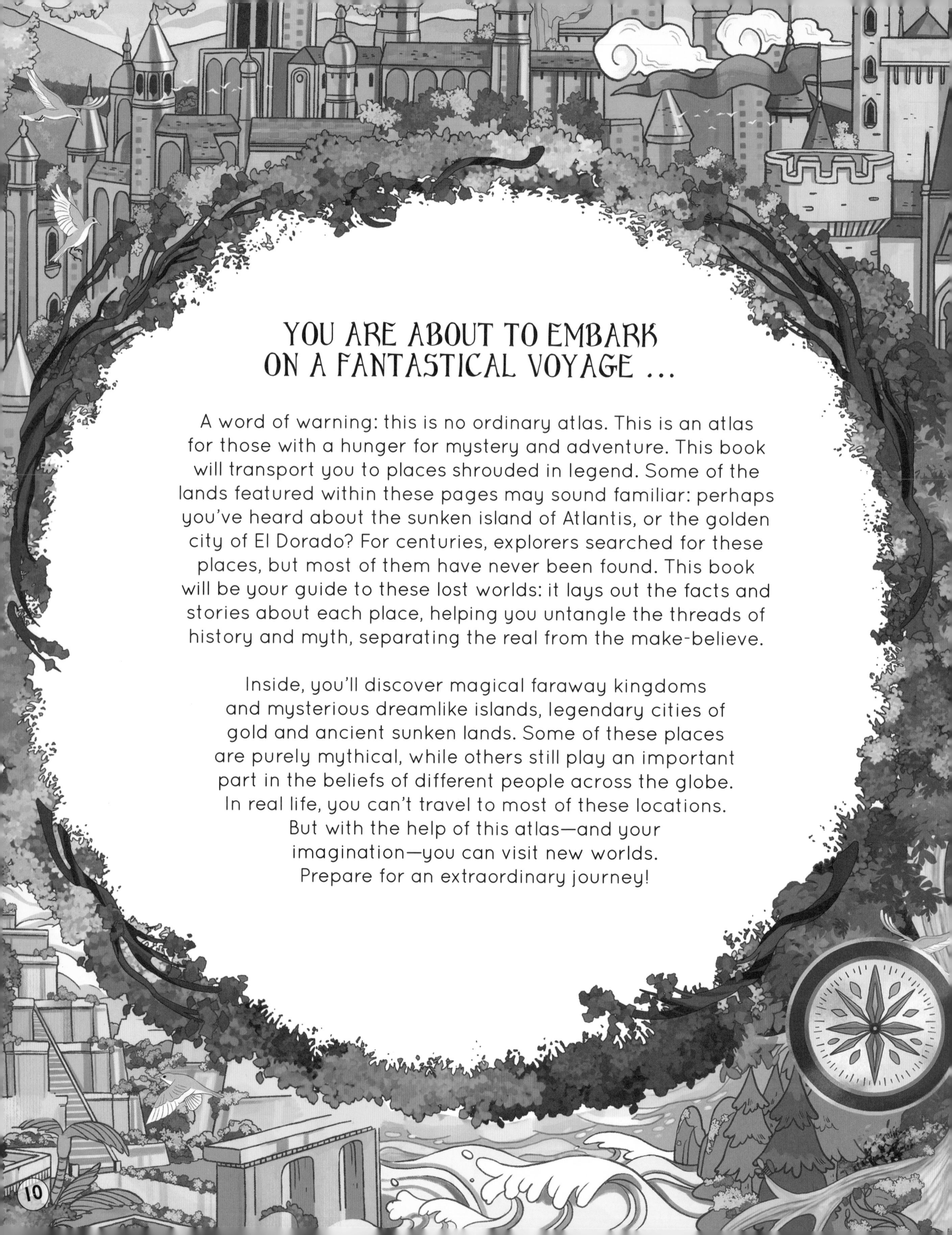

YOU ARE ABOUT TO EMBARK ON A FANTASTICAL VOYAGE ...

A word of warning: this is no ordinary atlas. This is an atlas for those with a hunger for mystery and adventure. This book will transport you to places shrouded in legend. Some of the lands featured within these pages may sound familiar: perhaps you've heard about the sunken island of Atlantis, or the golden city of El Dorado? For centuries, explorers searched for these places, but most of them have never been found. This book will be your guide to these lost worlds: it lays out the facts and stories about each place, helping you untangle the threads of history and myth, separating the real from the make-believe.

Inside, you'll discover magical faraway kingdoms and mysterious dreamlike islands, legendary cities of gold and ancient sunken lands. Some of these places are purely mythical, while others still play an important part in the beliefs of different people across the globe. In real life, you can't travel to most of these locations. But with the help of this atlas—and your imagination—you can visit new worlds. Prepare for an extraordinary journey!

Sunken Lands and Phantom Islands

Around the world and through the ages, tales of sunken lands have been told in many different cultures, from ancient Greece to the Mayan Empire, from the myths of Indigenous Americans to stories from the remote Solomon Islands. These tales may have been inspired by real places that were submerged by rising waters, or dragged beneath the sea by earthquakes. Alongside these sunken lands, these pages also reveal many phantom islands: places that used to appear on maps, until geographers worked out that they never really existed. Most came about due to navigators' mistakes, or the vivid imaginations of sailors.

A Note on the Maps

Each chapter opens with a map revealing a selection of lost kingdoms and mythical lands from a particular continent. The maps aren't "real" in the strictest sense: they reveal a land of the imagination. They show the places associated with certain legends and stories, as well as the destinations sought by explorers and treasure-hunters over the centuries.

One Last Thought

As you flip through these pages, consider this ...
There are some ancient cities (such as Troy) that were once thought to be mere legends, but whose remains have been discovered by modern archaeologists. How many more lost kingdoms, do you think, remain buried beneath the ground or under the sea, just waiting to be discovered?

THULE: The farthest north of all lands, believed to exist by some ancient Greeks and Romans
YGGDRASIL: The Nine Worlds of the Northlands
FRISLAND: Fake island that appeared on maps from the 16th century, claimed to have been discovered by explorers from Venice
NORWAY
SWEDEN
GREAT BRITAIN
CAMELOT: Many-towered castle of King Arthur
DENMARK
HY-BRASIL: Phantom island off the Irish coast
IRELAND
JASCONIUS: Imaginary island on the back of a sea monster, from the Irish legend of St. Brendan
BUYAN: Vanishing island from Slavic folklore
LOST CITY OF YS: Legendary kingdom swallowed by the sea
FRANCE
GERMANY
ATLANTIS: Legendary sunken city
COCKAIGNE: A dreamland of plenty and luxury
SARDINIA
MEDITERRANEAN SEA
ATLANTIC OCEAN
SPAIN
LAMOS: Island-home of man-eating giants, the Laestrygonians, from ancient Greek myths
PILLARS OF HERCULES
THE FORTUNATE ISLES: Paradise islands from Greek mythology

EUROPE

The famous lost kingdom of Atlantis was just one of the legendary lands imagined by the ancient Greeks. There were many others, from the blissful Fortunate Isles to faraway countries of giants and monsters. But beyond the Greeks, other tales from across Europe tell of mysterious cities steeped in legend. Some of the places shown here are purely mythical; others existed once, but have long since been lost or destroyed.

ATLANTIS: LEGENDARY SUNKEN CITY

Can a city be swallowed by the sea in a single night? According to an age-old legend, that is exactly what happened to the kingdom of Atlantis. The word "Atlantis" is steeped in mystery, conjuring images of ruined underwater temples, where shoals of fish dart between ancient statues and crumbling pillars. But does this sunken city really exist? Some people think this vanished island is one of history's greatest unsolved puzzles; others believe it is just a myth.

THE IDEA THAT A CITY COULD BE WIPED OUT BY A NATURAL DISASTER IS QUITE BELIEVABLE. THE ANCIENT CITY OF HERACLEION IN EGYPT WAS DESTROYED BY EARTHQUAKES AND TSUNAMIS.

THE ANCIENT GREEK SCHOLAR PLATO SAID THAT ATLANTIS LAY BEYOND THE "PILLARS OF HERCULES"—AN AREA THAT WE NOW CALL THE STRAIT OF GIBRALTAR.

CANALS AND BRIDGES

According to legend, the capital city of Atlantis was made up of two rings of land, one inside the other, linked by bridges over canals. In the center lay an island with a temple dedicated to the powerful sea god Poseidon.

AN ANCIENT TALE

Atlantis was first mentioned nearly 2,500 years ago by the ancient Greek philosopher Plato. He described a kingdom said to have existed 9,000 years before his time. In the tale, the island of Atlantis controlled an empire stretching from the Atlantic across the Mediterranean Sea. Its capital city was a wealthy port, home to lavish palaces, golden temples, and grand canals. The citizens were good and happy at first, but over time they grew wicked and greedy, so the gods decided to punish them. One night, they sent an earthquake to shake the city to its foundations. Then came a series of enormous waves that swallowed the ruins of this once-mighty kingdom, dragging the remains into the ocean depths.

Looking for Atlantis

The Atlantis legend has captivated people for centuries, and many places have been suggested as possible locations. Some think Atlantis was the Greek island of Santorini, which erupted in a huge volcanic explosion about 3,600 years ago. However, the timings of the eruption don't fit with Plato's story. Others say that the mountain tops of the sunken kingdom are the Azores Islands in the Atlantic. But no evidence of a once-great city has been discovered here.

The places marked here have all been suggested as locations for Atlantis, but none of them exactly matches Plato's description.

Fact or Fiction?

Most experts agree that Atlantis was never a real place, but was dreamed up by Plato as a fable. After all, it's unlikely such a city could have existed 9,000 years before Plato's time, when much of the world was still in the Stone Age. Whatever the truth of the matter, the tale of Atlantis certainly makes an enthralling story. And who knows? One day, underwater explorers might come across the remains of an ancient circular city, destroyed by an earthquake, beyond the Pillars of Hercules. Perhaps ...

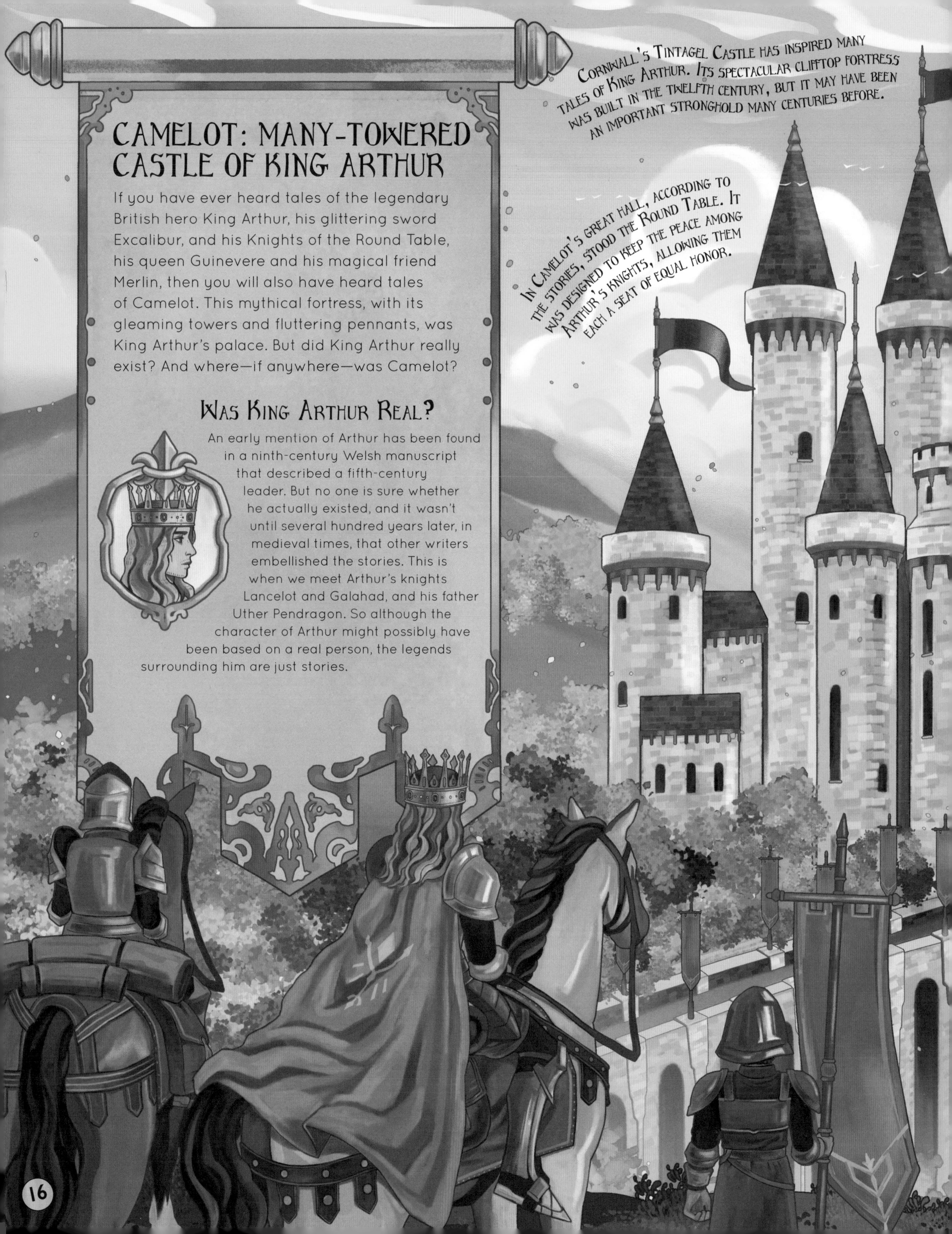

CAMELOT: MANY-TOWERED CASTLE OF KING ARTHUR

If you have ever heard tales of the legendary British hero King Arthur, his glittering sword Excalibur, and his Knights of the Round Table, his queen Guinevere and his magical friend Merlin, then you will also have heard tales of Camelot. This mythical fortress, with its gleaming towers and fluttering pennants, was King Arthur's palace. But did King Arthur really exist? And where—if anywhere—was Camelot?

Was King Arthur Real?

An early mention of Arthur has been found in a ninth-century Welsh manuscript that described a fifth-century leader. But no one is sure whether he actually existed, and it wasn't until several hundred years later, in medieval times, that other writers embellished the stories. This is when we meet Arthur's knights Lancelot and Galahad, and his father Uther Pendragon. So although the character of Arthur might possibly have been based on a real person, the legends surrounding him are just stories.

Cornwall's Tintagel Castle has inspired many tales of King Arthur. Its spectacular clifftop fortress was built in the twelfth century, but it may have been an important stronghold many centuries before.

In Camelot's great hall, according to the stories, stood the Round Table. It was designed to keep the peace among Arthur's knights, allowing them each a seat of equal honor.

The Sword in the Stone

Long ago, so the story goes, Britain was ruled by Uther Pendragon. His queen had a baby boy, Prince Arthur. But these were dangerous times, and Uther's adviser, the wizard Merlin, warned the king that the baby was not safe in the castle. Arthur was sent away to be brought up in the countryside. No one, not even Arthur himself, knew his true identity.

Years later, the king and queen died and the land was plunged into chaos. The nobles argued about who should rule, trouble-makers went unpunished and people lived in fear. No one remembered the king's son … except Merlin. Merlin used his magic to embed a beautiful sword in a stone outside the palace. The weapon was engraved with these words: "Whosoever shall pull this sword from the stone is the one true king."

One by one, the contenders stepped up, eager to prove themselves—but they couldn't budge the sword an inch. But that day, who should happen to be passing but the 15-year-old Arthur? Drawn by the commotion, he shouldered through the crowd to try his luck.

On his first attempt, to the amazement of all watching, he slid out the sword as if it were the easiest thing in the world. And so the young prince became a king, and tales of his adventures are still told to this day.

Finding Camelot

Most people believe Camelot is fictional. But if Arthur was a real historical figure, he would have had a base somewhere. This map shows sites in Wales and England that have been suggested as possible locations for Camelot.

HY-BRASIL: PHANTOM ISLAND OFF THE IRISH COAST

For many years people in Ireland have talked of a mysterious land named Hy-Brasil, said to lie off the country's western shores, in the Atlantic Ocean. According to local legends, this strange place is usually cloaked in fog, impossible to see. However, on one day every seven years, the misty veil is drawn aside, revealing a beautiful landscape of mountains and green fields. Riches, fame, and even eternal life could await any brave sailor bold enough to set foot on this puzzle of an island, so the stories say ...

On the Map

In the past, mapmakers included Hy-Brasil on their charts. It first appears on an Italian map from 1330. It crops up on countless maps after this, sometimes shifting location, sometimes changing shape, sometimes with a slightly different name. In fact, it kept appearing on maps until about 1865. And then, it disappeared. Nowadays, there is no trace of the island. But did it ever really exist?

Hy-Brasil was often shown as a circle with a channel running through the middle from east to west. This shape may have been used by historic mapmakers to suggest they weren't sure whether a particular landmass was really there.

IRELAND

GREAT BRITAIN

If Hy-Brasil isn't real, then why was it ever drawn on maps?

Before the age of exploration, the Atlantic was an uncharted wilderness. Mapmakers may have believed that in such a vast ocean there must be many scattered islands, so perhaps they simply added these imagined places to their charts.

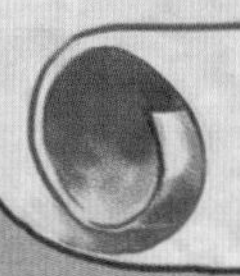

Setting Sail for Hy-Brasil

In 1480 a ship embarked from the English port of Bristol, manned by a crew of explorers determined to find the legendary island. However, the expedition ended in failure. The following year another ship set sail with the same goal—but again, the sailors returned home defeated. Through history, many have searched for this mysterious island, but there are no reliable records of it ever having been found. And the reason? Sadly, it was probably always just a figment of the imagination.

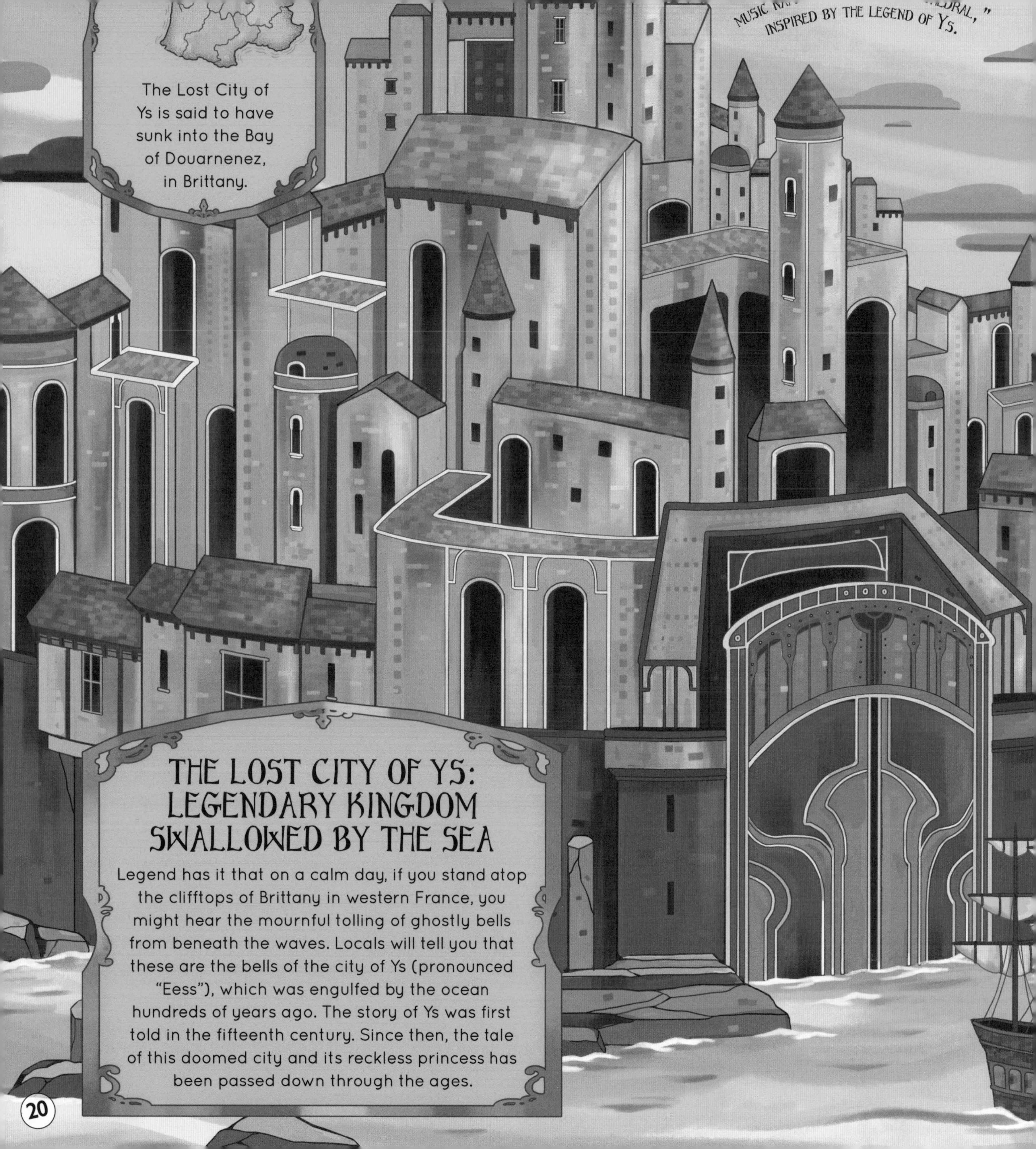

The Lost City of Ys is said to have sunk into the Bay of Douarnenez, in Brittany.

INSPIRED BY THE LEGEND OF YS.

THE LOST CITY OF YS: LEGENDARY KINGDOM SWALLOWED BY THE SEA

Legend has it that on a calm day, if you stand atop the clifftops of Brittany in western France, you might hear the mournful tolling of ghostly bells from beneath the waves. Locals will tell you that these are the bells of the city of Ys (pronounced “Eess”), which was engulfed by the ocean hundreds of years ago. The story of Ys was first told in the fifteenth century. Since then, the tale of this doomed city and its reckless princess has been passed down through the ages.

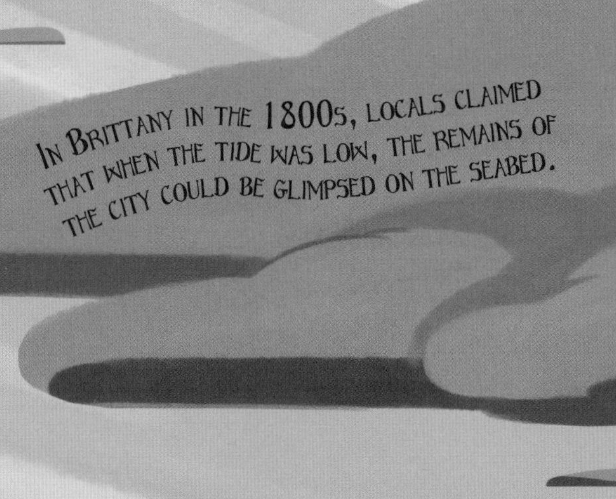

City of the Sea

According to the folk tales, long ago in Brittany there was a king called Gradlon. He doted on his only daughter, Dahut, who adored the wild ocean. Her chief desire was to live in a city as close to the shore as possible, so Gradlon granted her wish. A grand city was constructed on the coast, with a palace made of marble and gold. Around the town a huge sea wall was built, complete with strong floodgates to keep the waters at bay. At low tide these were unlocked to allow ships in and out. There was only one key to the gates, which the king kept safe on a gold chain around his neck. For a while, the city thrived. Its fine streets thronged with artists, scholars, merchants, and traders.

Princess Dahut

The story goes that Gradlon was a good man, but Dahut was wilful and wayward, rebelling against her father. One night, she sneaked into his chamber as he slept, lifting the key from around his neck. She ran to the sea wall to open the gates for her sweetheart's ship. But that night the tide was high. Paralyzed with horror, Dahut looked on from the watchtower as the swirling waters rushed through the gates and flooded the city. King Gradlon managed to escape on his magic horse, seizing up his daughter on the way. But as they galloped over the crashing waves, Dahut slipped and fell into the ocean depths. Some say that she was transformed into a mermaid, and if you listen carefully, you might still catch her sorrowful song on the ocean breeze.

Strong Girls

This story is similar to the legend of Atlantis, but it also echoes other ancient tales: those of headstrong women who bring chaos through their wickedness or disobedience. Thankfully, times have changed, and the stories we tell have changed too. Nowadays of course, strength and independence are prized in girls far above unquestioning obedience. And perhaps the idea of being turned into a mermaid isn't too awful a fate after all!

YGGDRASIL: THE NINE WORLDS OF THE NORTHLANDS

Long ago, the Norse people of Scandinavia believed that at the center of the universe was a great tree, called Yggdrasil. Among its sturdy branches nestled nine different worlds. Asgard, home of the high gods, was at the top, while our human world lay in the middle. Elsewhere among the branches were the worlds of the Hidden Folk: magical beings such as elves, dwarves, and giants. Around the roots slithered the mighty serpent Nidhogg, and at the base lived three sisters called the Norns, who watered the tree.

Alfheim

Alfheim was the home of the elves, who were even more radiant than the sun. These bright, beautiful folk could be kind to humans but were quick to anger, so the Norse people often left them gifts to keep them happy.

Midgard

The human world—known as Midgard, the "Middle Land"—was at the center of the world tree. Above it lived the gods, below it lay the underworld, and all around was a wild, deep ocean inhabited by a fearsome sea monster.

Jotunheim

Among the enemies of the gods were the frost giants, who lived in the mountainous world of Jotunheim. Their king Thrym was lord of this wild, rugged place. The giants were often violent but were also wise, and they loved riddles.

Niflheim

Nothing lived in this mysterious realm of mist, ice, and snow, but here lay one of the three wells that watered the world tree itself.

The Norse World

The Norse myths were common across Scandinavia and Germany. Midgard was the known world, but the other eight—stretching into the heavens or deep into the earth—are trickier to show on a map!

Asgard

Connected to Midgard via a rainbow bridge was Asgard: home of the Aesir, the high gods. From this celestial land the great lord Odin could survey all the Nine Worlds. And it was here, in the hall of Valhalla, that the souls of noble warriors were thought to end up.

Vanaheim

Vanaheim was home to the Vanir—the old gods of nature, fertility, and magic. This was a beautiful, wild place of forests and fields. In Vanaheim's grand mead halls the old gods held their councils.

Svartalfheim

The world of the dwarves was known for its underground labyrinths, lit only by the glow of flaming torches and blazing furnaces. The dwarves were blacksmiths who crafted many magical objects, including the hammer of the thunder god Thor, as well as Odin's spear.

Muspelheim

A land of fire, Muspelheim was the realm of the warlike fire giants. The stories foretold that at the end of time, there would be a great battle called Ragnarok. When this reckoning came, the flaming lord Surt would break free from Muspelheim and rain fire and terror down on Asgard.

Hel

This shadowy realm lay beneath the roots of the world tree, ruled over by Hel, goddess of the dead. In the Norse tales, this wasn't a place of torment for wicked people—it was the final destination for any Northlander who didn't die in battle.

COCKAIGNE: A DREAMLAND OF PLENTY AND LUXURY

If you could invent an imaginary land, what would it look like? Perhaps the houses would be built from candy, cakes would grow on trees and fountains would overflow with hot cocoa? In medieval Europe, about 700 years ago, this kind of place was dreamed up by peasants who worked in the fields. Their lives were hard, so they told stories of a paradise where mouth-watering food was plentiful and no one had to work. This place was named Cockaigne, which meant "the land of cake."

In French Cockaigne the rivers flowed with wine, while in the Italian version sausages grew on vines and there was a mountain made of Parmesan.

Often, tales of this earthly paradise featured edible buildings ... not so practical when it rained, but then again, it never rained—it only drizzled custard.

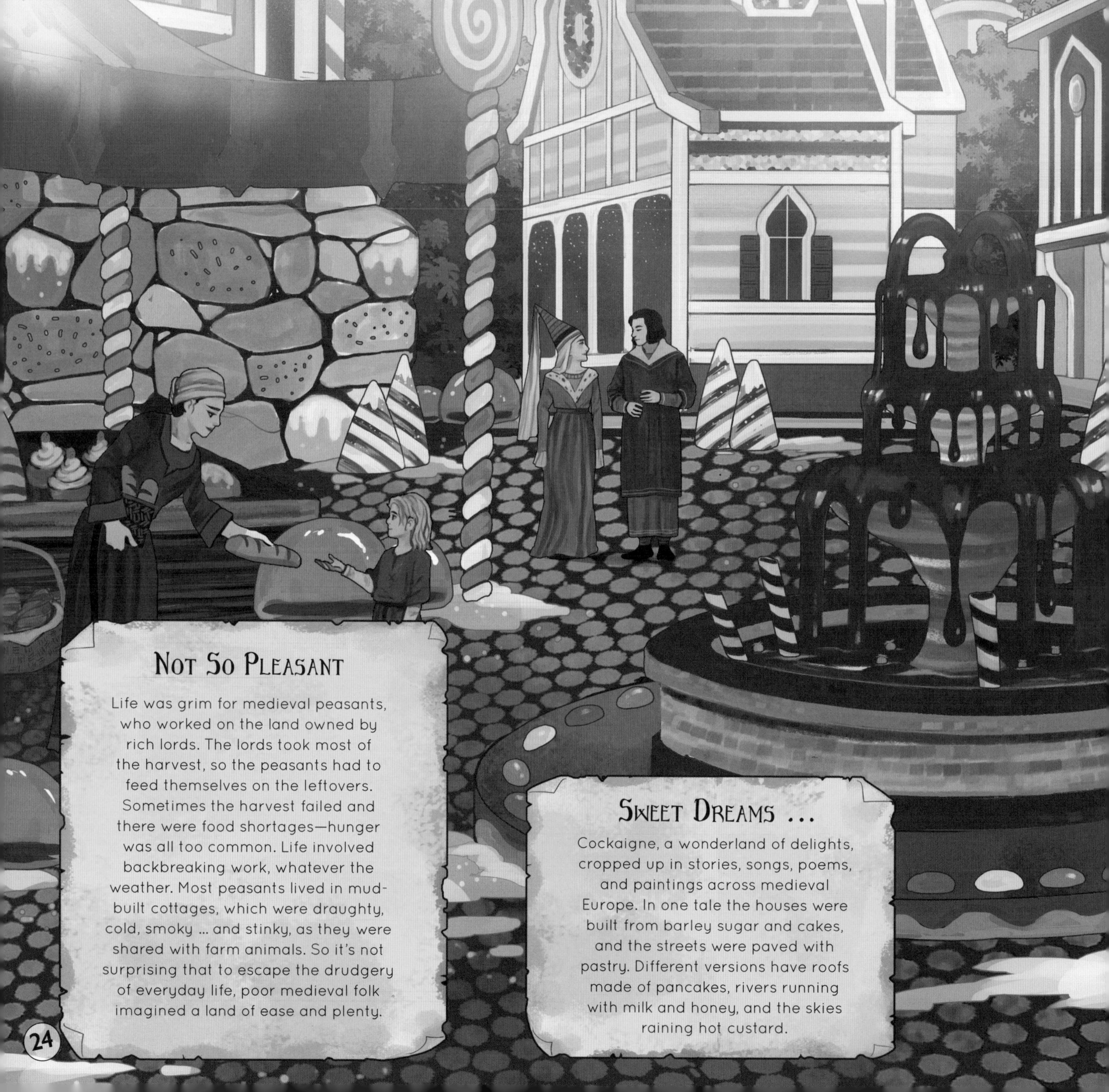

Not So Pleasant

Life was grim for medieval peasants, who worked on the land owned by rich lords. The lords took most of the harvest, so the peasants had to feed themselves on the leftovers. Sometimes the harvest failed and there were food shortages—hunger was all too common. Life involved backbreaking work, whatever the weather. Most peasants lived in mud-built cottages, which were draughty, cold, smoky ... and stinky, as they were shared with farm animals. So it's not surprising that to escape the drudgery of everyday life, poor medieval folk imagined a land of ease and plenty.

Sweet Dreams ...

Cockaigne, a wonderland of delights, cropped up in stories, songs, poems, and paintings across medieval Europe. In one tale the houses were built from barley sugar and cakes, and the streets were paved with pastry. Different versions have roofs made of pancakes, rivers running with milk and honey, and the skies raining hot custard.

... Meat Dreams

Meat was a luxury, so many visions of Cockaigne seem obsessed with it. Stories talk of roast geese wandering the streets, hams growing on trees, houses made of meat pies, and cooked fish leaping out of the water, ready to eat. In pictures, roast pigs trot along with knives handily wedged in their sides, for ease of slicing!

Finding Cockaigne

A poem from 1350 said Cockaigne lay to the west of Spain. However, sadly, it wasn't somewhere that could really be reached. Even at the time, it's likely no one actually believed Cockaigne was a real place. But we can still dream!

A Lazy Life

In contrast to a peasant's grueling work day, in this dreamland you didn't have to do anything but lounge around and play games. Everything was easy and comfortable: there was no nighttime, no danger, and no death. There were no flies, no fleas, and no lice. There wasn't even any arguing. But with food that flew straight into your mouth, and no work to do, there was nothing to argue about!

THE FORTUNATE ISLES: PARADISE ISLANDS FROM GREEK MYTHOLOGY

The ancient Greeks believed that somewhere in the vast ocean to the west of Europe, just beyond the horizon, lay the Fortunate Isles. According to the myths, when you died you ended up in the underworld. But if you were one of the lucky few—a heroic warrior, or someone who'd lived a virtuous life—then you might spend eternity on these paradise islands. This idea of a distant land of happiness, peace and plenty has been passed down through the years and appears in many tales from around the world.

Heaven on Earth

The Fortunate Isles were reserved for the souls of the Greek heroes and a few lucky mortals specially favored by the gods. On these sun-kissed shores, the trees dripped with honey-sweet fruit and the air was filled with birdsong and the scent of flowers. The weather was warm, but there were shady groves and ocean breezes to keep everyone at just the right temperature. The deserving few could laze around on soft beds of moss, dabbling their fingers in crystal streams of water while congratulating themselves on being among the chosen ones.

Ancient poems and stories sometimes call these islands the Isles of the Blessed, Elysium, or the Elysian Fields.

The story of Hy-Brasil (see page 18) and Cockaigne (see page 24), as well as many other mythical islands, were probably inspired by tales of the Fortunate Isles.

Mapping Paradise

The Fortunate Isles are mythical, but long ago some believed they had a real location. According to the writings of the Greek poet Homer, from about 3,000 years ago, they lay at the western edge of the Earth on the banks of the great river Oceanus, which encircled the world. Later writers described them as lying 10,000 furlongs (about 1,200 miles) away from Africa, or a few days' sail away from Spain. In medieval times, before people really knew what lay in the uncharted ocean west of Europe, mapmakers added the Fortunate Isles to their charts. They were often positioned near the Canary Islands.

What Lies Beyond?

The Greeks saw the Atlantic Ocean as a wild, unknowable place; the border between their world and the mysterious realm beyond. For as long as we can remember, people have been curious about what lies out of reach, just over the horizon. When we don't know exactly what's out there we imagine things, which is why the Greeks dreamed up a perfect paradise just beyond the setting sun.

BUYAN: VANISHING ISLAND FROM SLAVIC FOLKLORE

"Far, far away, in the Ocean-Sea, on the island of Buyan ..." This is how many Slavic folk tales begin. The Slavic people—who have lived in Russia, Central, and Eastern Europe since the sixth century—have a rich and varied folklore, in which this mysterious island plays an important part. Like other legendary isles from around the world, this puzzling place is difficult to find, seemingly appearing and disappearing at random. The home of many fantastical beasts, Buyan is described as lying at the center of everything—the place from where the sacred world tree grows.

The World Tree

Just as the Norse people believed in the mighty tree Yggdrasil, the Slavic people also pictured a great world tree, in which gods, humans, and strange creatures all had a place. This oak tree, so the stories tell us, was rooted on the magical island of Buyan, connecting the heavens to the underworld.

Koschei the Deathless

This hideous folklore villain is the stuff of nightmares. A powerful sorcerer, Koschei is fond of kidnapping princesses. However old and skeletal he becomes, he can never die because his soul doesn't dwell inside his body. Instead, he keeps his soul hidden far away on the island of Buyan, trapped inside an egg, hidden inside a locked chest, buried under the sacred oak tree.

In some stories Buyan is the resting place of the Alatyr Stone: a magical stone with healing power said to sit at the center of the universe.

Another resident of the island is the Indrik, king of beasts. This mythical creature has the body of a bull, the head of a horse, the legs of a deer, and the horn of a unicorn. It is powerful enough to trigger an earthquake just by rolling over!
The Slavic World
In most of the stories Buyan was a magical, otherworldly place whose location couldn't be pinned down on any map. But some have wondered whether the Baltic island of Rügen, at the edge of the Slavic world, might have inspired the tales.
Russia
Rügen
Belarus
Poland
Ukraine
Czechia
Slovakia
Some say that the Alatyr Stone lies beneath the world tree, guarded by the iron-beaked bird Gagana and the serpent Garafena.

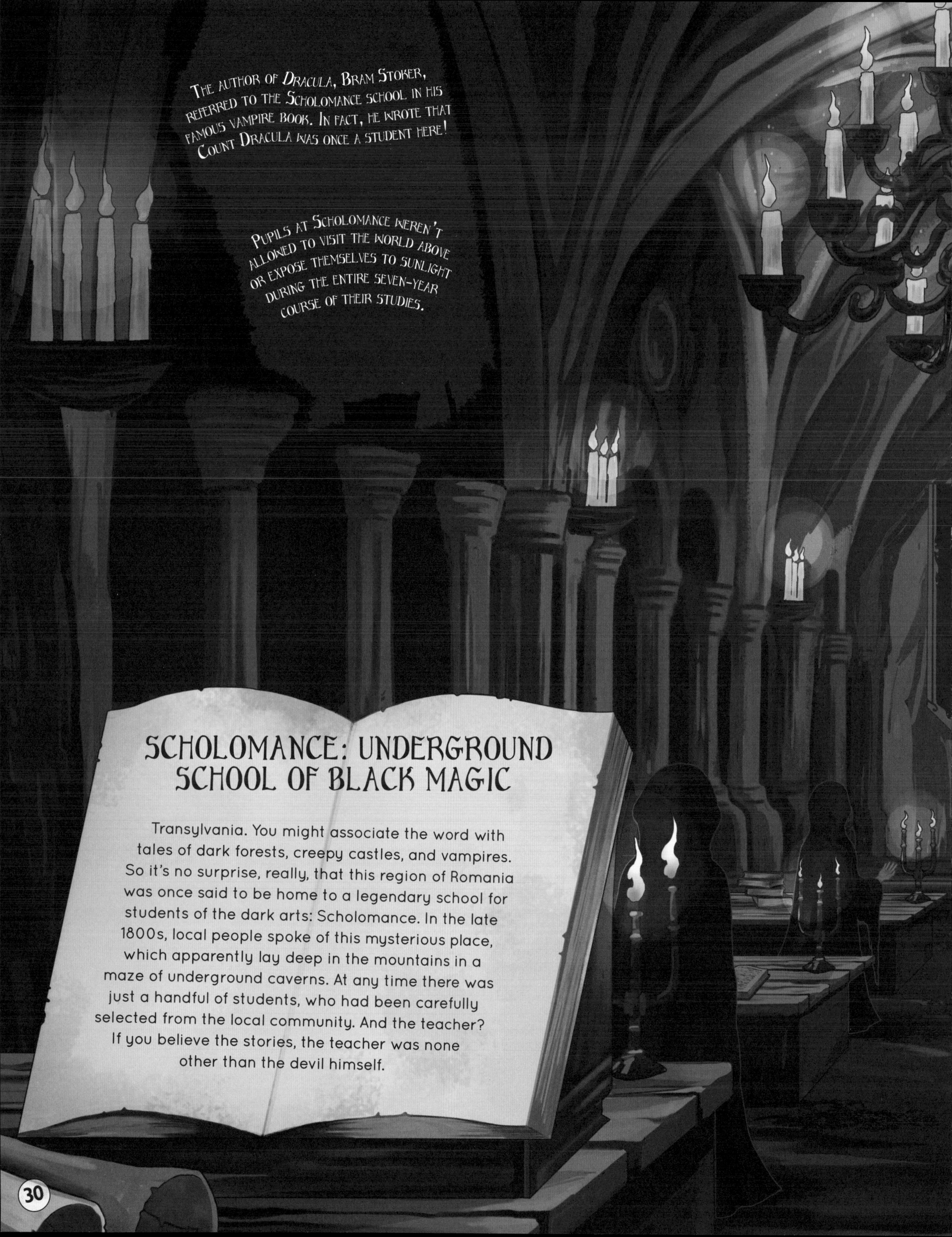

The author of *Dracula*, Bram Stoker, referred to the Scholomance school in his famous vampire book. In fact, he wrote that Count Dracula was once a student here!

Pupils at Scholomance weren't allowed to visit the world above or expose themselves to sunlight during the entire seven-year course of their studies.

SCHOLOMANCE: UNDERGROUND SCHOOL OF BLACK MAGIC

Transylvania. You might associate the word with tales of dark forests, creepy castles, and vampires. So it's no surprise, really, that this region of Romania was once said to be home to a legendary school for students of the dark arts: Scholomance. In the late 1800s, local people spoke of this mysterious place, which apparently lay deep in the mountains in a maze of underground caverns. At any time there was just a handful of students, who had been carefully selected from the local community. And the teacher? If you believe the stories, the teacher was none other than the devil himself.

Dragon-Riders

Students learnt to cast spells, shapeshift, talk to animals, control the weather, and ride dragons. After seven years of study, one student would be chosen to become one of the "Solomnari." These powerful wizards brewed thunderbolts in a mountaintop lake, then rode a storm dragon across the sky, unleashing thunder, lightning, rain, and hail. In fair weather, so the stories said, the dragon rested in the depths of the lake. Locals warned against throwing stones into the waters for fear of rousing the beast and triggering a thunderstorm. The Solomnari were said to roam the countryside dressed as beggars, carrying a magic bag containing a book of spells, a golden dragon bridle, and an iron axe for shattering ice-clouds to make hail.

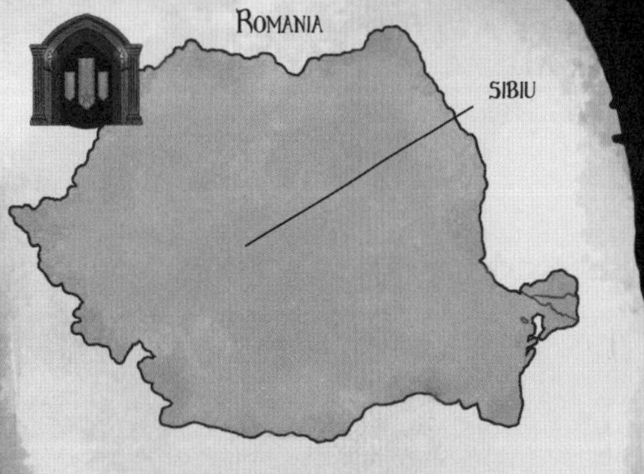

Romania

Sibiu

Scholomance was reported to lie deep under the Transylvanian Alps, near the town of Sibiu. Of course, no such underground school has been discovered in real life ... yet!

SIJILMASA: Once one of the most important oasis cities in Africa; now just ruins remain
MOROCCO
TUNISIA
CARTHAGE: Once-great rival of Rome
LIBYA
RUINED CITADEL OF DJADO: Abandoned trading outpost in the Sahara Desert
ZERZURA: The Oasis of Little Bird
NORTH ATLANTIC OCEAN
MALI
NIANI: Now-vanished capital of the once-powerful Mali Empire
ILE-IFE: Sacred homeland of the Yoruba people
NIGERIA
ST. MATTHEW ISLAND: Non-existent island once thought to lie in the Atlantic; appeared on maps from the 16th century
NAMIBIA
SOUTH ATLANTIC OCEAN
THE LOST CITY OF THE KALAHARI: Fact or fiction?

Libertatia: Pirates' paradise once thought to have existed in Madagascar

Mapungubwe: Lost medieval kingdom of South Africa

South Africa

Juan de Lisboa: Fabled island said to have been discovered by the Portuguese; appeared on maps from the 17th century

AFRICA

This vast continent has inspired many tales of lost kingdoms. The legendary oasis of Zerzura was once thought to lie hidden amid the sands of the Sahara, while the Lost City of the Kalahari was believed to exist in the deserts of southern Africa. As well as these lost kingdoms, this map reveals strange islands that have vanished from modern charts, ancient capitals of legendary queens, and once-great cities whose ruins lie undiscovered.

ZERZURA: THE OASIS OF LITTLE BIRDS

The scorching sands of the Sahara stretch for thousands of miles across north Africa. Since early times, travelers in this inhospitable landscape have faced blistering temperatures, blinding sandstorms, and shifting dunes. So it's no surprise that many who ventured into the desert did not return: stories tell of the Sahara swallowing people, camel-trains, and even entire armies. But of the countless legends that swirl around this vast desert, none are quite so intriguing as the story of the lost oasis of Zerzura.

West of the Nile

Egyptian and European explorers believed that the lost city lay in Egypt or Libya, southeast of a vast area of dunes called the Great Sand Sea.

Ancient Rumors

Zerzura was mentioned in a fifteenth-century Arabic manuscript called *The Book of Hidden Pearls*. This guide for medieval treasure-hunters described a whitewashed city in the desert, above whose gate was carved a stone bird. The book claimed that behind the door, treasure-seekers would find riches, as well as a sleeping king and queen, who should not be woken. It sounds like a fairy tale, but in the 1800s an English Egyptologist heard further reports of Zerzura. Apparently a local man had stumbled across the city while out looking for a lost camel. He told of ancient ruins surrounded by palm trees, olive groves, and bubbling springs of water.

One of the first people to cross the eastern Sahara was the Egyptian explorer and mapmaker Ahmed Hassanein. In 1923 he made an extraordinary 2,200-mile journey by camel.

The Zerzura Club

In the past, much of the Sahara was uncharted. But in the 1920s and 30s, new technology helped mapmakers travel farther into the desert than ever before. Some fitted crawler tracks to cars to help them navigate the terrain; others scouted the area using aircraft. The Zerzura Club, founded in 1930, was a group of European explorers intent on discovering the lost city. Flying over the desert in 1932, they spotted a green valley in a rocky plateau called the Gilf Kebir. Could this be Zerzura, they wondered? Later, the Hungarian adventurer Count László Almásy explored the valley on foot, but found no ruins, and no treasure. However, he did find some 9,000-year-old rock paintings of graceful swimming figures, suggesting that perhaps this area was once much greener than it is now, dotted with lakes and rivers.

Just a Mirage?

These days, the expanse of the Sahara has been explored and mapped: from the ground, from the air, and also from space, using satellites. Although there are many ruins of abandoned desert towns, no treasure-filled ancient city has been discovered matching Zerzura's description. But as with many "lost" cities, it's difficult to *prove* that Zerzura doesn't exist. Even if it is just a myth, its legend will no doubt live on—a tantalizing mirage tempting anyone with a thirst for adventure.

SHEBA: KINGDOM OF AN ANCIENT QUEEN

Have you ever heard of the Queen of Sheba? Tales of this ancient leader have been passed down for thousands of years: she is mentioned in the Bible and the Quran, and is celebrated in art and music. But did she really exist? And where, exactly, was Sheba? In the Bible we're told that the queen visited King Solomon of Israel in Jerusalem, leading a grand procession carrying gold, frankincense, and precious stones. So Sheba must have been a place rich in gold, where frankincense trees grew. Experts have narrowed it down to two contenders: Yemen on the Arabian Peninsula, and Ethiopia on the Horn of Africa.

MANY ETHIOPIANS BELIEVE THAT THEIR KINGS WERE DESCENDED FROM THE QUEEN OF SHEBA, WHOSE DYNASTY LASTED 3,000 YEARS UNTIL THE DEATH OF EMPEROR HAILE SELASSIE IN 1975.

HISTORIANS DON'T AGREE ON WHETHER THE QUEEN OF SHEBA WAS A REAL PERSON—THIS MYSTERIOUS CHARACTER REMAINS A PUZZLE.

AN ETHIOPIAN LEGEND

Many Ethiopians see the Queen of Sheba as the mother of their nation. The *Kebra Nagast* is a sacred Ethiopian book from medieval times, which claims the queen was a powerful ruler called Makeda. This clever, adventurous woman apparently visited King Solomon and later bore his child, Menelik. When Menelik grew up he traveled to Jerusalem to meet his father, then—so the story goes—he returned home with some very precious cargo ...

THE ARK OF THE COVENANT

This ancient chest is one of the world's most famous lost treasures. According to the Bible, it held the stone tablets upon which the Ten Commandments were engraved. The Ark's location is a centuries-old mystery, but in Ethiopia many claim to know what happened to it. The *Kebra Nagast* says the Ark was brought to Ethiopia from Jerusalem by the Queen of Sheba's son. In the town of Aksum, there is a church where the Ark is still said to lie. It is guarded by a monk—the Guardian of the Ark—who has devoted his life to protect it. Except for the Guardian no one is allowed to see the Ark, let alone examine it, so historians will probably never know whether there is any truth to the legend.

Kingdom of Aksum

Aksum was an Ethiopian kingdom that grew powerful about 2,000 years ago. This area was rich in precious jewels, gold, and spices, and was an important hub on the trade routes between India and the Roman Empire. In modern-day Aksum lie the ruins of a historic palace: could this, perhaps, have been the home of the Queen of Sheba? Although archaeologists have dated the ruins to 1,000 years later than she supposedly lived, they have discovered a gold mine here, which could explain the ancient queen's famous riches.

Where was Sheba?

Although Ethiopia has a strong claim, some historians say that Sheba was actually the kingdom of Saba, based in Marib in modern-day Yemen. Others argue that the kingdom of Sheba stretched across the Red Sea, encompassing parts of both Yemen and Ethiopia.

THE LOST CITY OF THE KALAHARI: FACT OR FICTION?

The Kalahari Desert is an expanse of sand and shrubland spanning parts of Botswana, Namibia and South Africa. This vast, dry wilderness is not somewhere you would expect to find many ancient ruins. But in 1885 a Canadian man named William Leonard Hunt crossed the Kalahari with a group of local guides. After the expedition, he claimed to have found huge stone walls half-buried by the desert sands, which he believed were the remains of a historic city. Was Hunt correct, or could there be another explanation for these mysterious stones?

A Needle in a Haystack

Hunt's story caused quite a stir, and in the years that followed many expeditions set out to track down the lost city. In 1949 the South African air force sent planes over the Kalahari to search for traces from above, and recently people have used satellite images to scan the desert for clues. But although Hunt described the ruins in detail, his notes about their exact location are unclear. So far, the only evidence for the city is Hunt's own story.

THE HAND OF NATURE?

Hunt described finding a wall made of large, flat-sided stones. But experts have suggested that perhaps it was not built by humans, but by nature. There is a type of volcanic rock found in this area called dolerite. Dolerite rocks formed millions of years ago when lava erupted from beneath the Earth's crust. The lava cooled, shrinking and cracking to create strange, straight-sided blocks. Some even have grooves between them that look just like the gaps in a stone wall!

IF THERE WAS AN ANCIENT CITY IN THE KALAHARI, IT MIGHT HAVE HAD LINKS WITH GREAT ZIMBABWE. THIS 900-YEAR-OLD SETTLEMENT WAS BUILT BY THE SHONA PEOPLE IN ZIMBABWE. IT HAD THICK STONE WALLS, EMBELLISHED WITH TOWERS.

THE GREAT FARINI

William Leonard Hunt was not a typical explorer. In his youth, he shot to fame as a tightrope walker known as the Great Farini. In the 1860s he performed daredevil stunts, such as turning somersaults on a high-wire above Niagara Falls. He even invented the human cannonball trick!

THE SEARCH CONTINUES?

Although it's highly unlikely that the Lost City of the Kalahari exists, there's a small possibility that there is something out there, buried beneath the shifting sands. But it's worth remembering that William Hunt was a showman at heart. Perhaps the Lost City was never real, and was instead the last spectacular illusion of the Great Farini.

CARTHAGE: ONCE-GREAT RIVAL OF ROME

About 2,500 years ago, if you had sailed along the coast of Tunisia in north Africa, you would have been awed by the majestic walls of Carthage rising from the sea. At one time, Carthage was a hugely powerful city, described as the jewel of the western Mediterranean. Its large navy controlled a vast area, making it a thorn in the side of the emerging Roman Empire. Eventually, a series of wars with Rome led to Carthage's downfall. It was besieged, stormed, and burned by the merciless Roman army. Today only the ruins of this once-mighty city remain, but the stories live on.

Two famous names will forever be linked to the city of Carthage. One is the real-life general Hannibal, and the other is the legendary queen Dido ...

Dido

Historians don't agree on whether Dido (also known as Elissa) was a real person or just a myth. According to the tales, Dido was princess of the Phoenician city of Tyre, but was forced to flee from her murderous brother. She sailed to north Africa, where she asked the local king for some land. The king allowed her only as much land as could be enclosed by the skin of a single ox. Clever Dido cut the skin into thin strips, laid them end to end, and measured out an area big enough to build a kingdom on ... the kingdom of Carthage.

Hannibal

This Carthaginian military leader was a great enemy of Rome. In 218 BCE he famously attacked the Roman Empire by marching his army of 40,000 men, 9,000 horses, and 37 elephants through Spain and France, then over the Alps. He is also known for tying flaming torches to the horns of oxen to create a diversion so his army could get away under the cover of darkness. And he catapulted poisonous snakes onto the ships of his opponents!

Phoenician City

The Phoenician people, whose civilization flourished about 3,000 years ago, originally lived along the coast of what are now Lebanon, Syria, and Israel. They were skilled seafarers who set up trading ports across the Mediterranean. Carthage was a Phoenician port founded in modern-day Tunisia. The city grew quickly, becoming wealthy and powerful, with a strong navy. Carthage was famed for its grand city walls, marble buildings, palatial gardens, and twin harbors. In its busy marketplace, merchants, sailors, and traders from across Africa, Europe, and Asia would have mingled.

ILE-IFE: SACRED HOMELAND OF THE YORUBA PEOPLE

In southwestern Nigeria lies Ile-Ife: a real city with a legendary backstory. According to the traditional religion of the Yoruba people, from western Africa, Ile-Ife is the place where all life began. In the beginning, so the Yoruba stories tell us, the universe consisted of only the heavens, the dark sea, and the marshes. In the heavens lived the all-powerful god Olodumare. One day, Olodumare gave his son Obatala an important job to do: he asked him to create the land. But things didn't quite go according to plan...

1. Obatala Begins

Obatala was excited to be given such a special task and set about gathering everything he would need: a long gold chain, a snail shell full of sand, a palm seed, and an enormous cockerel. As Obatala was making his way to the Earth, he passed some of the other gods having a party. They invited Obatala to have a drink with them. "Just one drink shouldn't hold me up too much," thought Obatala. But he ended up having so much wine that he fell into a deep sleep.

Where is Ile-Ife?

The kingdom of Ile-Ife is a real place that flourished between the eleventh and the fifteenth centuries as a center for trade, art, and culture. The city survives to this day.

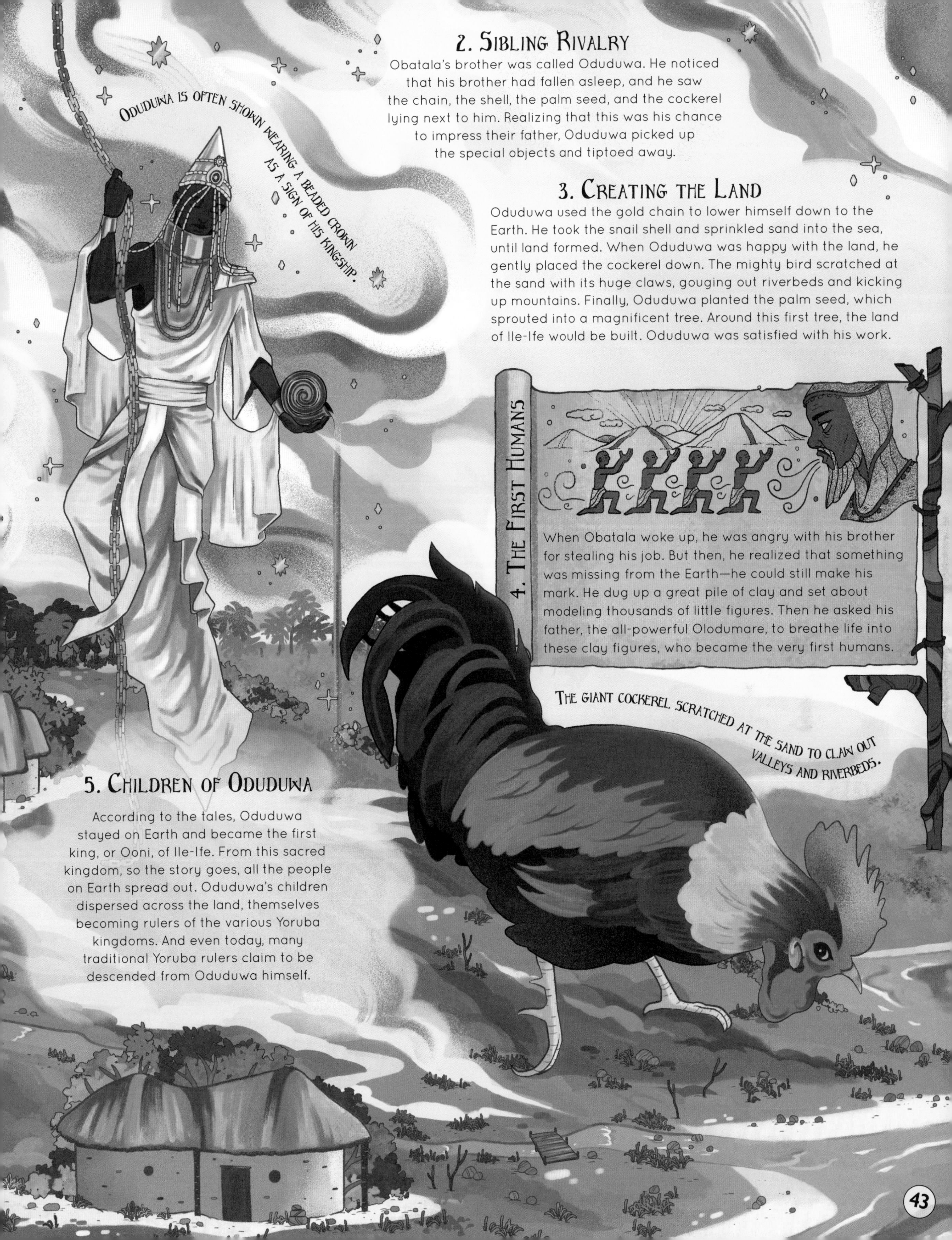

2. Sibling Rivalry

Obatala's brother was called Oduduwa. He noticed that his brother had fallen asleep, and he saw the chain, the shell, the palm seed, and the cockerel lying next to him. Realizing that this was his chance to impress their father, Oduduwa picked up the special objects and tiptoed away.

3. Creating the Land

Oduduwa used the gold chain to lower himself down to the Earth. He took the snail shell and sprinkled sand into the sea, until land formed. When Oduduwa was happy with the land, he gently placed the cockerel down. The mighty bird scratched at the sand with its huge claws, gouging out riverbeds and kicking up mountains. Finally, Oduduwa planted the palm seed, which sprouted into a magnificent tree. Around this first tree, the land of Ile-Ife would be built. Oduduwa was satisfied with his work.

4. The First Humans

When Obatala woke up, he was angry with his brother for stealing his job. But then, he realized that something was missing from the Earth—he could still make his mark. He dug up a great pile of clay and set about modeling thousands of little figures. Then he asked his father, the all-powerful Olodumare, to breathe life into these clay figures, who became the very first humans.

5. Children of Oduduwa

According to the tales, Oduduwa stayed on Earth and became the first king, or Ooni, of Ile-Ife. From this sacred kingdom, so the story goes, all the people on Earth spread out. Oduduwa's children dispersed across the land, themselves becoming rulers of the various Yoruba kingdoms. And even today, many traditional Yoruba rulers claim to be descended from Oduduwa himself.

Lake Issyk-Kul: Ancient folk tales describe a sunken city lost beneath the waters of this lake
Kyrgyzstan
Turquoise Mountain: Lost Central Asian city destroyed in the 13th century by the son of the warrior Genghis Khan
Themiscyra: Capital of the Amazons
Troy: City of legend
Black Sea
Turkey
Iraq
Afghanistan
Hufaidh: Magical disappearing island once believed to exist in the marshes of southern Iraq
Dwarka: Legendary home of a Hindu god
Hanging Gardens of Babylon: Lost wonder of the world
Oman
India
Iram of the Pillars: The Atlantis of the Sands
Ram Setu: Limestone bridge between India and Sri Lanka, said to have been built by warrior monkeys for the Hindu god Rama
Indian Ocean

Asia

The largest continent in the world is home to countless cultures and languages, with a rich history stretching back thousands of years. It's not surprising, then, that Asia is full of lost kingdoms, from the historic citadel of Troy—a city at the heart of a world-famous story—to legendary desert oases and now-vanished wonders of the world. You may also find disappearing islands, mythical underwater lands, and a real-life sunken city!

TROY: CITY OF LEGEND

The legend of the Trojan War is one of the most famous stories ever told. This tale of love and strife, of gods and heroes, was set down by the Greek poet Homer about 3,000 years ago. But how much, if any, of the story is based on history? And did the city of Troy ever exist?

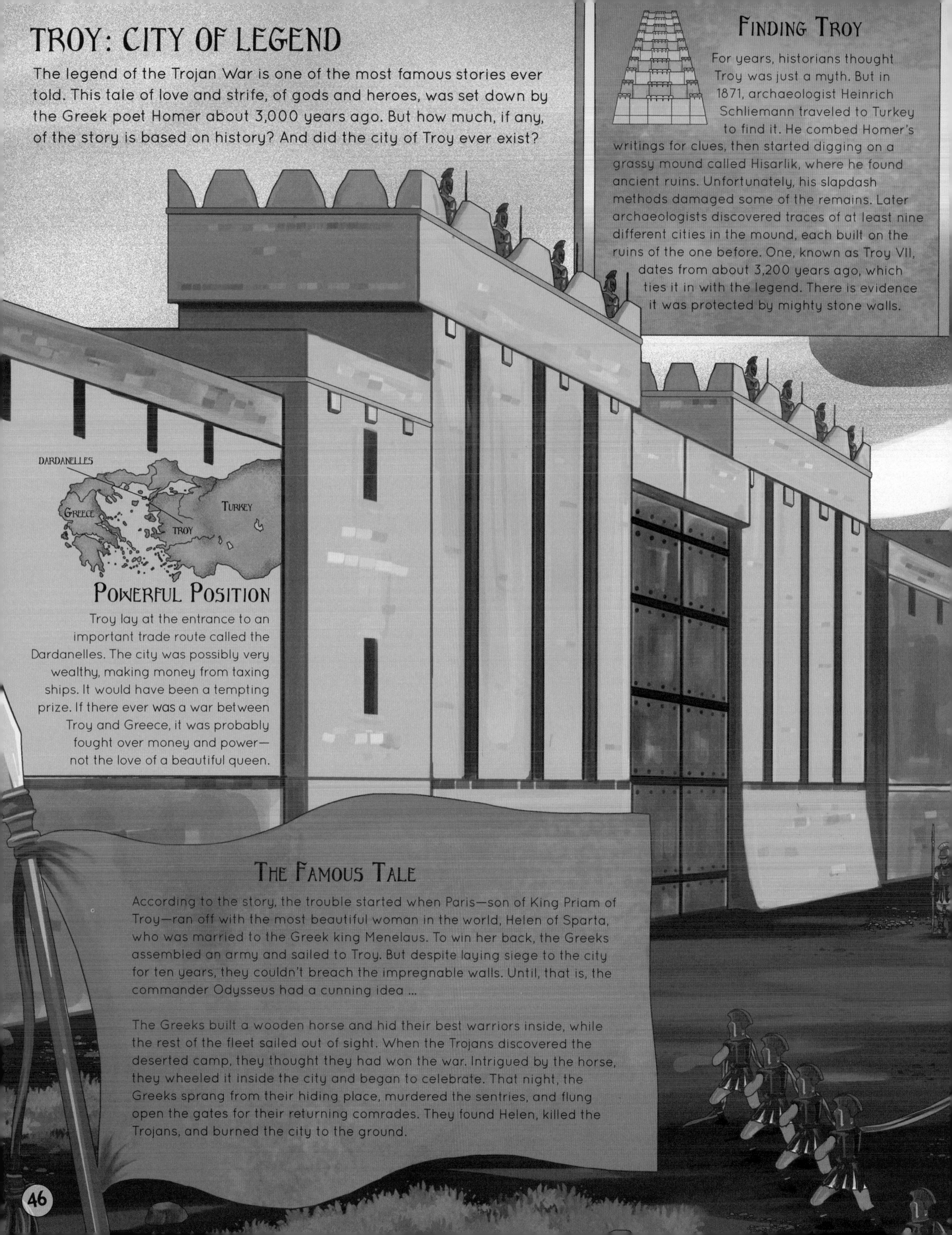

Finding Troy

For years, historians thought Troy was just a myth. But in 1871, archaeologist Heinrich Schliemann traveled to Turkey to find it. He combed Homer's writings for clues, then started digging on a grassy mound called Hisarlik, where he found ancient ruins. Unfortunately, his slapdash methods damaged some of the remains. Later archaeologists discovered traces of at least nine different cities in the mound, each built on the ruins of the one before. One, known as Troy VII, dates from about 3,200 years ago, which ties it in with the legend. There is evidence it was protected by mighty stone walls.

Powerful Position

Troy lay at the entrance to an important trade route called the Dardanelles. The city was possibly very wealthy, making money from taxing ships. It would have been a tempting prize. If there ever was a war between Troy and Greece, it was probably fought over money and power—not the love of a beautiful queen.

The Famous Tale

According to the story, the trouble started when Paris—son of King Priam of Troy—ran off with the most beautiful woman in the world, Helen of Sparta, who was married to the Greek king Menelaus. To win her back, the Greeks assembled an army and sailed to Troy. But despite laying siege to the city for ten years, they couldn't breach the impregnable walls. Until, that is, the commander Odysseus had a cunning idea ...

The Greeks built a wooden horse and hid their best warriors inside, while the rest of the fleet sailed out of sight. When the Trojans discovered the deserted camp, they thought they had won the war. Intrigued by the horse, they wheeled it inside the city and began to celebrate. That night, the Greeks sprang from their hiding place, murdered the sentries, and flung open the gates for their returning comrades. They found Helen, killed the Trojans, and burned the city to the ground.

Fact or Fiction?

Today most historians agree that Troy was a real place. At Hisarlik archaeologists have found arrowheads, skeletons of people who met grisly ends, and signs of fire damage. There are clues that people once lived cramped together, stockpiling food, lending a grain of truth to the tale of a city under siege. But most of the legends around Troy—Paris and Helen, Achilles and Hector—are probably just stories; stories that continue to captivate us to this day.

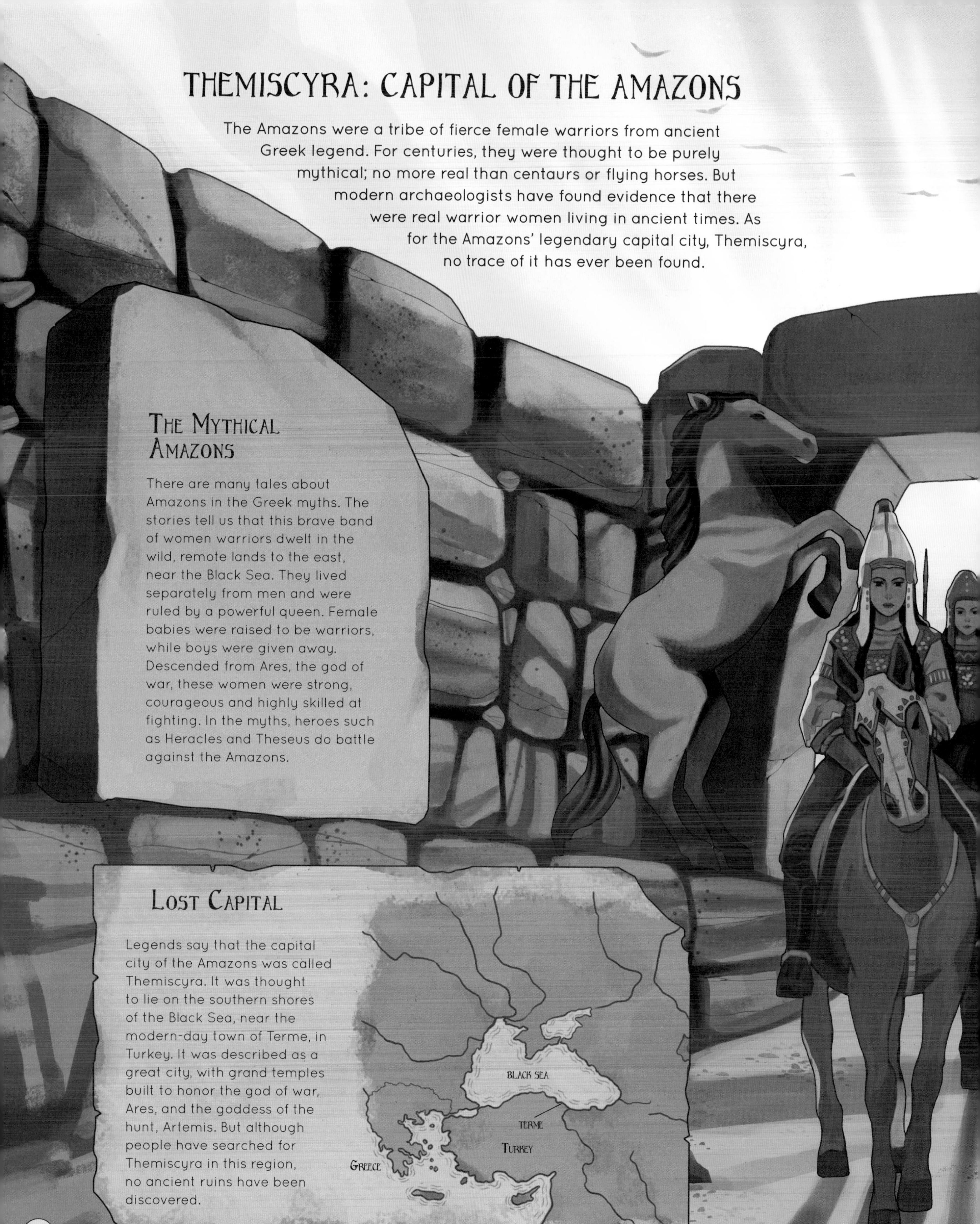

THEMISCYRA: CAPITAL OF THE AMAZONS

The Amazons were a tribe of fierce female warriors from ancient Greek legend. For centuries, they were thought to be purely mythical; no more real than centaurs or flying horses. But modern archaeologists have found evidence that there were real warrior women living in ancient times. As for the Amazons' legendary capital city, Themiscyra, no trace of it has ever been found.

The Mythical Amazons

There are many tales about Amazons in the Greek myths. The stories tell us that this brave band of women warriors dwelt in the wild, remote lands to the east, near the Black Sea. They lived separately from men and were ruled by a powerful queen. Female babies were raised to be warriors, while boys were given away. Descended from Ares, the god of war, these women were strong, courageous and highly skilled at fighting. In the myths, heroes such as Heracles and Theseus do battle against the Amazons.

Lost Capital

Legends say that the capital city of the Amazons was called Themiscyra. It was thought to lie on the southern shores of the Black Sea, near the modern-day town of Terme, in Turkey. It was described as a great city, with grand temples built to honor the god of war, Ares, and the goddess of the hunt, Artemis. But although people have searched for Themiscyra in this region, no ancient ruins have been discovered.

The Real Amazons?

It's possible that stories of the Amazons were based on the real-life Scythian people. These tribes of horseback warriors lived in Central Asia about 2,500 years ago. Scythian women were treated equally to men, and were trained to fight: they rode horses, threw spears, and fired arrows. They even wore pants, which was very unusual in those days! In recent years, archaeologists have explored ancient burial mounds in Russia and Ukraine. They unearthed the remains of several female Scythians who had been given a warrior's burial, laid to rest alongside their daggers and quivers of arrows. Although Scythian women didn't live separately to men, you can easily see how these female warriors might have inspired the Greeks' stories.

THE HANGING GARDENS OF BABYLON: LOST WONDER OF THE WORLD

The Hanging Gardens of Babylon were one of the Seven Wonders of the Ancient World. Age-old writings describe these lush gardens towering over the sun-baked landscape. Terraces were stacked on top of terraces, bursting with fragrant plants to delight all who laid eyes on them. But despite many years of searching, no remains of the gardens have been found. In fact, we can't say for sure if they even existed at all. Today, this elusive wonder remains one of history's best-kept secrets.

Gardens of Legend

Babylon, once one of the largest cities on Earth, lay in western Asia in what is now Iraq. In the fourth or fifth century, a Greek named Philo wrote a handbook describing Seven Wonders of the World, among which he listed the Hanging Gardens of Babylon. It's said that these leafy terraces were built more than 2,500 years ago in the reign of King Nebuchadnezzar II. The story goes that he made them for his wife, Amytis, who missed the green mountains of her Persian homeland. The gardens were said to have many terraces held aloft by stone columns, thickly planted with trees and flowers.

Searching for Clues

Many ancient writers talked about these spectacular gardens. But the problem is, there is not a word about them in any records from Babylon itself. And even though the city ruins have been carefully excavated, no evidence of the gardens has been unearthed. Descriptions say the lower terrace stretched for 390 feet in each direction, and the upper terrace was 80 feet above the ground. These gardens were big. So why can't we find them? Were the tales just based on rumors? Or is there another explanation?

Jewel of Nineveh?

Some historians think the gardens were never in Babylon at all, but lay 310 miles to the north in the city of Nineveh. The confusion, they say, can be blamed on ancient Greek writers getting confused over their geography! Stone carvings from Nineveh talk about a raised garden that was a "wonder for all peoples." And archaeologists have found the remains of ancient aqueducts in the area, which would explain how the plants were watered.

Thirsty Work

Experts say that in such a dry area, the gardens would have needed up to 330 tons of water every day—that's about 75,000 bucketfuls! According to carvings in Nineveh, the gardens had an impressive system of pipes to raise water from the river. Inside each pipe was a spiral blade. When the blade was turned, the spiral scooped up water and passed it up the cylinder to the terraces above. This type of machine is known as an Archimedes Screw (even though it was dreamed up several hundred years before the life of the Greek inventor).

The gardens were said to have been cleverly designed, with terraces lined with tar and lead to make them leak-proof.

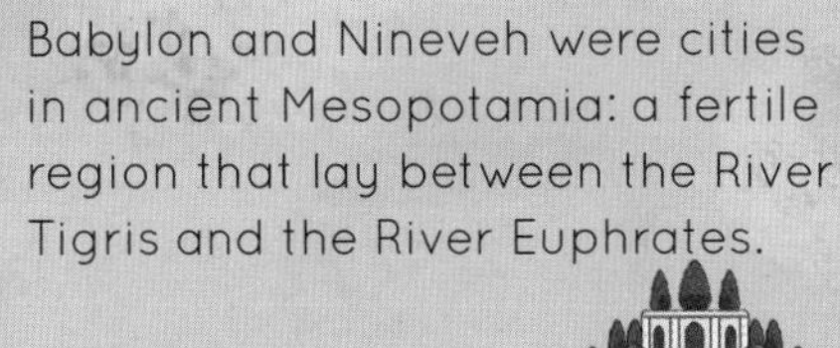

Babylon and Nineveh were cities in ancient Mesopotamia: a fertile region that lay between the River Tigris and the River Euphrates.

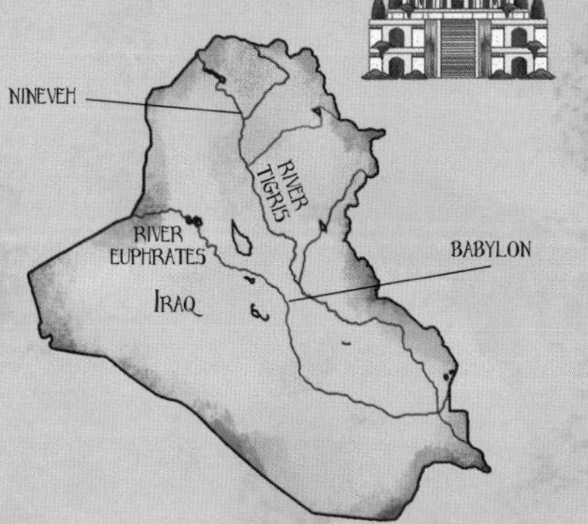

IRAM OF THE PILLARS: THE ATLANTIS OF THE SANDS

This mysterious city, once thought to have been lost beneath the majestic dunes of the Arabian Desert, is mentioned in the Quran, the holy book of Islam. We're told that the wicked citizens of Iram turned away from Allah, the one true god, and received a divine punishment. A roaring wind arrived, lasting for seven nights and eight days, and the city was swallowed by the swirling sands. The road was blotted out, and the place became a distant memory. For centuries, people have wondered if the tale is simply a fable intended to teach its listeners a lesson ... or whether it was based on a real place.

One Thousand and One Nights

Iram of the Pillars also makes an appearance in a collection of Middle Eastern folk tales called *Alf Laylah wa-Laylah*, or *One Thousand and One Nights*. In this story, King Shaddad commands the building of a great city, with palaces made of silver and gold, gates inlaid with jewels, and balconies overlooking burbling rivers. Such was the beauty of the place that it took three hundred years to build. King Shaddad—who miraculously was still alive at this point—was on his way to visit his new city when the whole place was destroyed by God, to punish the king for his pride and vanity.

Seeking the City

In the early twentieth century the city was sought by explorers who had heard rumors about it from local Bedouin tribespeople. But after many had tried and failed to find it, Iram—also called Ubar—was dismissed as a myth. And then, in 1992, an expedition team used satellite pictures to discover the ruins of a buried settlement in southern Oman. They unearthed a hidden fortress, with crumbling walls and the remains of several towers, as well as pieces of pottery dating back 4,000 years! The team believed they had found the lost city, which, they said, had once been an important stopping-off point for desert travelers. Instead of being buried by a sandstorm, the fortress had collapsed into a huge sinkhole.

Lost No Longer?

Was this buried fortress really the lost city of Iram, or was it a relic from another more modest trading town? The walls measured just 180 by 210 feet: too small to have contained a large settlement. Scientists say this barren part of the Arabian Desert—known as Rub' al Khali, or the Empty Quarter—was far too dry, even thousands of years ago, to support a big city. Just like the flying carpet or Aladdin's magic lamp—more stars from *One Thousand and One Nights*—this lost city of silver and gold was probably always just a story.

Ancient tales describe Iram—or Ubar—as a wealthy city with beautiful gardens, fountains, and "lofty pillars."

Location of the Lost City?

A ruined fortress was discovered in this remote part of Oman in 1992 ... but it probably wasn't the grand city of legend.

This legendary lost city was called the "Atlantis of the Sands" by the British army officer T.E. Lawrence (also known as Lawrence of Arabia).

DWARKA: LEGENDARY HOME OF A HINDU GOD

The modern-day town of Dwarka lies on the west coast of India. It's one of the seven sacred cities of the Hindu religion, with thousands of visitors flocking to its famous Dwarkadhish Temple every year. According to Hindu beliefs, an ancient city was founded here long ago by the god Krishna. It is said that the god reclaimed a piece of land from the sea, directing the building of palaces and gardens. But 5,000 years ago, so the story goes, Krishna's city was swallowed by the ocean.

Krishna's golden city of Dwarka is mentioned several times in a sacred Hindu text, the Mahabharata.

In Hindu mythology, the gods can have different identities, or "avatars." Krishna is seen as an avatar of the Lord Vishnu, the protector of the universe.

Where is Dwarka?

Sacred City

In a historic manuscript written around the ninth century in the ancient Sanskrit language, Krishna's city is described in the most extravagant terms. It was said to have 900,000 palaces, each built from crystal and silver, and adorned with gold and precious jewels. Lotus flowers bloomed in the beautiful lakes, where the calls of swans and cranes could be heard. The grand streets were lined with assembly houses and temples to the gods, while above them, brightly colored banners fluttered in the breeze. Another ancient Hindu text, the *Mahabharata*, says that when the god Krishna departed from the Earth, the oceans rose up and engulfed the city.

Ancient Remains?

So is this drowned city just a legend, or is there any truth to the stories? In the 1980s Indian archaeologists claimed to have discovered the remains of an ancient underwater city off the coast near modern-day Dwarka. The team declared they had found ruined city walls, anchors, and pieces of pottery dating back 3,500 years. But not everybody is convinced that the ruins are quite so old. More recently, marine archaeologists have suggested that the submerged remains are, in fact, not a whole ancient city, but harbor jetties from the fifteenth century, when sea levels were lower.

The legends say that one of Krishna's palaces had pillars built from coral, walls bedecked with sapphires, and canopies made from strings of pearls.

Krishna's city was said to have been filled with the sounds of birds singing as they flitted around the beautiful parks and pleasure gardens.

SHI CHENG: REAL-LIFE SUNKEN CITY

In the east of China lies the Qiandao Reservoir. The blue waters of this vast lake are dotted with green hillocks of all sizes, giving it the nickname the Lake of a Thousand Islands. But 60 years ago, these islands were actually the tops of mountains. In 1959 a hydroelectric power station was built on the banks of the River Xin'an, and a huge area was flooded to create an artificial lake. To make way for the lake, thousands of people were forced to move and their homes disappeared underwater. But along with the modern-day towns and villages that were submerged, something much more ancient was hidden beneath the waters of the reservoir.

THE CITY'S STONE WALLS WERE PROBABLY BUILT DURING THE MING DYNASTY IN THE SIXTEENTH CENTURY.

PAIRS OF CARVED LIONS, SYMBOLS OF STRENGTH AND BRAVERY, ARE OFTEN FOUND AT THE ENTRANCES TO CHINESE TEMPLES AND PALACES.

WHAT LIES BENEATH

In 2001 a team of scuba divers found the remains of a historic city on the lake floor. In recent years, more divers have discovered paved boulevards, grand city walls, and imposing gateways adorned with intricate carvings of lions, dragons and other mythical creatures. This city—Shi Cheng—has been amazingly well preserved. Instead of being worn away by wind and rain, the ornate stonework is frozen in time, protected by the cool waters of the lake.

SHI CHENG LIES SUBMERGED UNDER 130 FEET OF WATER. AT THIS DEPTH, LITTLE SUNLIGHT FILTERS DOWN FROM ABOVE, SO DIVING TEAMS HAVE TO ILLUMINATE THE AREA WITH SPECIAL LANTERNS.

LION CITY

The city of Shi Cheng is thought to have been founded around 1,400 years ago in the time of the Tang Dynasty. It was built in the shadow of Five Lion Mountain. In fact, the name Shi Cheng means "Lion City" in Mandarin, which explains the carved lions that flank the now-silent streets. Once, this place was full of life, its streets bustling with horse-drawn carriages, ox-carts, and rickshaws, the air full of the calls of market-traders and the playful shrieks of children. But now the city's ghostly remains lie abandoned in the eerie stillness of this underwater world.

FINDING SHI CHENG
CHINA
QIANDAO RESERVOIR
SHI CHENG

XANADU: CAPITAL OF AN EMPIRE

In the thirteenth century, the powerful Mongol Empire stretched from eastern China all the way across Asia and into Europe. It was the largest empire the world had ever known. This superpower was commanded by the emperor Kublai Khan, the grandson of the fearsome horseback warrior Genghis Khan. In 1256 Kublai Khan founded a new city, which would become legendary for its luxury and grandeur. This city was called Shangdu, but in the west it became known by a different name: one that conjured images of exotic mystery ... Xanadu.

SHANGDU WAS POSITIONED TO BE IN HARMONY WITH ITS SURROUNDINGS, WITH THE MOUNTAINS TO THE NORTH, AND THE RIVER TO THE SOUTH. AROUND THE CITY, SHEEP AND GOATS GRAZED IN GREEN MEADOWS.

EMPEROR'S PLAYGROUND

Shangdu, or Xanadu, was the summer capital of the Mongol Empire: loved by the emperor for its cool breezes, shady forests, and lush grasslands. Inside the walled inner city was the majestic imperial palace, while the outer city contained barracks for soldiers, workshops, markets, taverns, and homes. The city was built on rolling grassy plains, which provided perfect hunting grounds. The emperor hosted hunting parties and grand feasts, with visitors coming from far and wide.

THE CITY WAS BUILT IN A SQUARE SHAPE, SURROUNDED BY 16-FOOT-HIGH WALLS, EACH WITH SIX WATCHTOWERS.

Ghost Town

Once, this city was home to more than 100,000 people, but in 1369 it was battered by warfare and later abandoned. People took away stones to build nearby towns and left the grass to grow over the remains. In the 1990s archaeologists began excavating the site, and it was opened to the public in 2011, but little is left of the city's original splendor. Only the ruins of the old earthen walls remain.

This map shows how far the Mongol Empire stretched in the thirteenth century. Shangdu lay in the north of what is now China, 220 miles north of present-day Beijing.

Marco Polo

One famous visitor was Marco Polo, who arrived in Shangdu in 1275. This European merchant and explorer had made a journey all the way from Venice in Italy across Asia at a time when such long-distance travel was unheard of. The magnificence of the city made an impression on Marco Polo, who later described it in his book *The Travels*. He spoke of a palace built from marble and stone, with rooms decked in gold, painted with exquisite murals of beasts and birds, trees and flowers. He recounted seeing a beautiful pavilion in the emperor's garden, colonnaded with gold pillars and carved with dragons.

RYŪGŪ-JŌ: UNDERWATER PALACE FROM JAPANESE LEGEND

Imagine a beautiful palace on the sea bed, deep beneath the ocean waves. To reach it, picture swimming through grand gates etched with golden dragons. Imagine the palace lying before you, its vast walls built from crystal, pearl, and coral, its roof laid with shimmering tiles. The ancient folk tales of Japan described such a palace. It was called Ryūgū-jō, and it was said to be the home of Ryūjin, the dragon-god of the sea.

King of the Sea

In Japanese myths, Ryūjin was king of dragons and lord of the ocean. Like the sea, the mood of this mighty serpent could turn in an instant, from calm and peaceful to wild and dangerous. He had the power to raise and lower the tides using magic jewels, and could unleash storms and tsunamis when stirred to anger. But he could also be kind, rescuing sailors lost at sea. He lived in the undersea palace of Ryūgū-jō with his daughter, Princess Otohime.

Locating the Legend

According to some of the legends, the undersea palace of Ryūgū-jō lay in the waters to the south of Japan's Kyushu Island.

The Tale of Urashima Tarō

This Japanese folk tale tells of a kind-hearted young fisherman, Urashima Tarō, who took a walk on the seashore one evening. He came across a group of boys beating a sea turtle with sticks. "Stop!" cried Urashima. "How could you?" But the boys carried on. "Here," insisted Urashima. "Take this money and leave the poor creature alone." The boys grabbed the money, shrugged, and ran off. "There you go, little one," said Urashima, lifting the turtle into the water. "You're safe now."

Next morning, Urashima set out in his boat. Soon, he heard his name being called. He looked overboard and was startled to see the turtle paddling alongside him.

"Urashima!" called the turtle. "You saved my life! How can I thank you? Would you like to travel with me to the palace of the sea king?" "I can't swim that far," laughed Urashima. But then, the turtle started to grow. It grew and grew until it was big enough for Urashima to ride on. Together, the pair plunged beneath the waves and journeyed all the way to the palace of Ryūgū-jō.

As soon as they arrived, the turtle transformed into a beautiful girl. "I am Princess Otohime," she said. "When you saved the life of that turtle, it was actually me you were saving." Urashima was entranced. He stayed in the Dragon Palace for three days, but eventually he grew homesick and decided it was time to return to his parents. Before he left, the princess gave him a mysterious jeweled box, but warned him never to open it.

When Urashima got back, everything was different. His home was nowhere to be found, and neither were his parents. He had been gone for much longer than he realized: not three days, but three hundred years! Distraught, he forgot the princess's warning and opened the box. A wisp of smoke escaped and encircled him. Within seconds, Urashima was transformed from a strong young lad into a stooped, ancient man, his face thin and lined. The box had contained Urashima's old age.

NORTH AMERICA

Through the ages, the spectacular mountains, forests, deserts, lakes, and icy expanses of North America have inspired tales of fantastical places. On this map you will find lost cities of gold, an ancient Viking town, phantom islands, and sacred places that have always held a special significance for Indigenous American people. Some of these places once existed, while others came to life only in stories ...

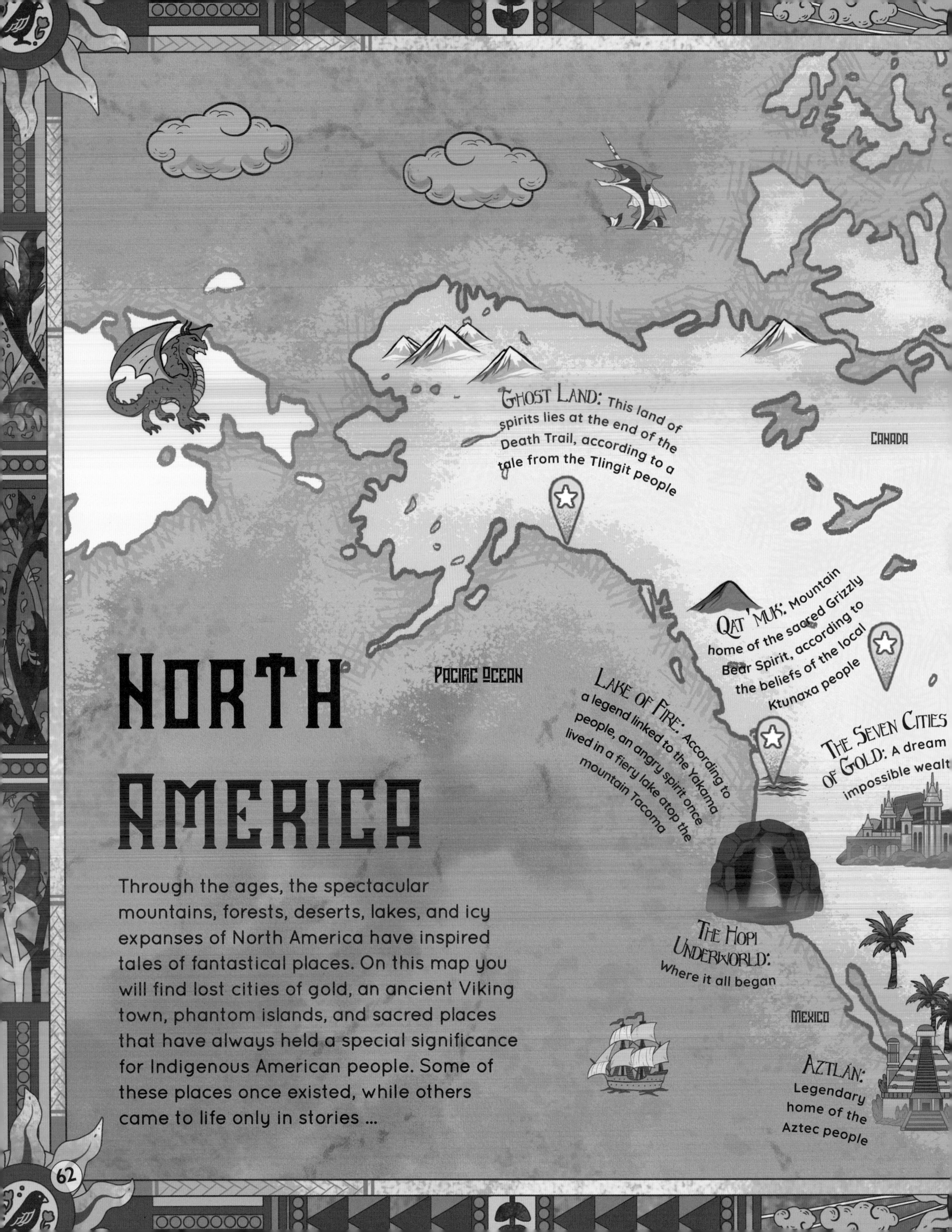

Akitsiraq: A secret stone circle said to mark a meeting place where a great council of Inuit leaders once met
Atlantic Ocean
Kingdom of Saguenay: Wealthy city in the north believed to exist by French explorers in the 16th century
The Isle of Demons: Phantom island off the coast of Canada
Satanazes: Island of Devils, according to 15th-century navigators' maps
Norumbega: Legendary Viking town that appeared on 16th-century maps (no trace of it has ever been found)
USA
Roanoke Colony: English settlement whose entire population mysteriously vanished in the 16th century
Antillia: Legendary island once thought to lie in the Atlantic Ocean, far to the west of Portugal and Spain
Bermeja: Mexican island that appeared on maps from the 16th century, but in 2009 was found not to exist

THE ISLE OF DEMONS: PHANTOM ISLAND OFF THE COAST OF CANADA

In the sixteenth and seventeenth centuries, a mysterious place called the Isle of Demons was drawn on maps of Newfoundland, in Canada. According to legend, it was named after the ghosts of drowned sailors who haunted its craggy cliffs. Mariners were said to be too afraid to land on the island. Instead, they sailed past at a safe distance, clutching their crucifixes in terror as they listened to the otherworldly wails that echoed from the misty shores. Even though these tales may have been exaggerated, there is, in fact, a real-life survival story linked to the Isle of Demons.

MAROONED!

In 1542 a French nobleman named Jean-Francois de Roberval took three ships full of supplies and settlers, and sailed from France to build a new colony in Canada. On board the ship the *Valentine* was his niece, Marguerite de La Rocque: a wealthy young noblewoman. During the voyage, Marguerite fell in love with one of the crewmembers. When her uncle found out, he was furious—he thought the affair would bring shame on the family. He ordered the ship to dock at the Isle of Demons, where Marguerite, her maid, and her sweetheart were set ashore and left to die.

WHERE WAS THE ISLE OF DEMONS?

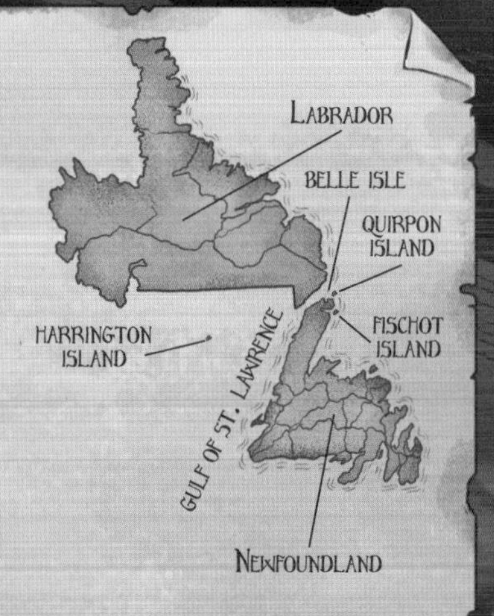

Although the story of Marguerite is probably based on truth, no one can say for sure where the Isle of Demons was. Some historians claim it may have been Fischot Island, whose colony of squawking gannets could explain the unearthly screeches reported by sailors! Others have suggested different Canadian islands as possible locations: Harrington Island, Quirpon Island, and Belle Isle are a few of the contenders.

Lone Survivor

The island, home to wolves and bears, was wild, windswept, and bone-chillingly cold. The trio had been left with scant supplies: they had a gun, a few knives, a small amount of food, and a tool for lighting fires. Together they managed to build a shelter, but before long both of Marguerite's companions had died. And so Marguerite—this young lady who had grown up accustomed to a life of ease and luxury—had to survive the wilderness alone. But survive she did: she gathered plants and hunted animals to eat, and she even shot a bear so she could wear its skin for warmth. After two gruelling years she spotted a boat in the distance and built a signal fire. At first the sailors were frightened, thinking this wild, fur-clad figure was a demon, but as they approached they were amazed by what they found. At last, this heroic survivor was rescued and taken back to France ... with quite a story to tell!

THE HOPI UNDERWORLD: WHERE IT ALL BEGAN

The Hopi people are a Indigenous American tribe from northeast Arizona, who have a history dating back thousands of years. According to the Hopi Way, the community has always been strongly connected with the land, seeing themselves as caretakers of the sacred Earth. In fact, according to Hopi beliefs, the people originally came from the very earth itself. Hopi legends tell of vast underground caverns where the first humans were created by the mother of all, Spider Woman.

The Creation Story

In the beginning, there was only the sun god, Tawa, and the Earth goddess, Spider Woman. They lived in the underworld. Above them there was no land, just an endless expanse of water. One day, the pair decided to make living things. Tawa sang a song of the beasts of the earth, the fish of the waters, and the birds of the sky. Then, Spider Woman took clay and molded these creatures. She placed a blanket over them and sang a magic song—and the animals' spirits awakened. Then, she took more clay and shaped it into human forms. She cradled these clay people in her arms, while she and Tawa sang the Song of Life. Finally, the humans breathed and stirred into being.

Then, Tawa went above and shone his fiery shield at the endless ocean, drying up the waters until the land appeared. Spider Woman led the people through the caverns of the underworld until they came to an opening, where the sun's rays beamed down from above. The goddess planted the seed of a reed, and the reed grew until it reached the opening in the roof of the cavern. Then, the people climbed up the reed ladder and spread out across the world. Spider Woman taught the people how to farm, and how to weave. And she reminded them to honor Mother Earth, from where they came, by always taking care of her.

Different Hopi groups have their own versions of the creation story. In another version, the first people take the form of ants, then wolves and bears, before becoming human.

Today, some Hopi ceremonies take place in sacred underground chambers called kivas. A kiva has a hole in the roof with a ladder reaching up to it, representing the journey of the Hopis' ancestors from the underworld.

Spider Woman's Hopi name is Gogyeng Sowuhti. This wise Earth goddess also appears in the mythologies of other Indigenous American nations, including the Navajo and Zuni people.
Spirals can be found in wall carvings and on Hopi pottery and jewelry. They symbolize the long journey made by the ancestors of the Hopi people.
Gateway Between Worlds
Arizona, USA
Grand Canyon
According to the legends, the opening from which the first people emerged was in the Grand Canyon, close to where the Colorado River meets the Little Colorado River. This portal was called a sipapu. Today, the Grand Canyon is still a sacred place for many Hopi people.

THE SEVEN CITIES OF GOLD: A DREAM OF IMPOSSIBLE WEALTH

A shipwreck. Four survivors. A tale of boundless treasure ... These all play their part in an extraordinary story: the story of the Seven Cities of Gold. It began hundreds of years ago in Portugal, when rumors started to fly of seven wealthy bishops who packed their ships with gold and sailed west across the ocean. When they landed, so the story goes, they built seven gleaming cities, famed for their riches. The legend of these cities of gold stayed alive through the ages.

Shipwreck Survivors

In the 1500s, Spanish and Portuguese invaders looted Central and South America, seizing land, gold, and silver. In 1527 a fleet left Spain intent on claiming what is now the US state of Florida. But eight years later, four weary travelers arrived in Mexico. They were the only survivors left from a crew of 600. The voyage had met with disaster after disaster, from shipwreck and starvation to capture by local Indigenous people. While describing their escape across the desert, the survivors also mentioned something else: a whispered rumor of gold. During their travels, so they said, the local tribes had talked of great cities in the desert to the northwest: cities that possessed vast riches.

The First Expedition

When news of these riches reached the Spanish authorities in Mexico, they pricked up their ears. Could these desert cities be the lost cities of gold? They planned an expedition to investigate. The expedition leader was a priest named Marcos de Niza, and the guide was one of the shipwrecked sailors: Estevanico, a Moroccan man who had been sold into slavery. The trip didn't go to plan: Estevanico was killed, and the priest turned back before reaching his goal. But on his return, he claimed to have seen a beautiful city from afar, with golden buildings ten stories high.

THE SEVEN CITIES OF GOLD WERE LEGENDARY PLACES THOUGHT TO BE HIDDEN IN THE DESERTS OF NEW MEXICO.

MARCOS DE NIZA CLAIMED TO HAVE SEEN A MAJESTIC DESERT CITY. DID HE LIE, OR MERELY EXAGGERATE? SOME HISTORIANS THINK HE MIGHT HAVE GLIMPSED A ZUNI SETTLEMENT AT SUNSET, WHEN THE SOFT LIGHT GAVE THE CLAY BUILDINGS A GOLDEN GLOW.

The Second Expedition

The priest's story electrified his listeners, and another search party was sent out, this time with the priest as a guide. The Spanish thought the cities lay in an area called Cibola, in what is now the US state of New Mexico. But when the explorers reached their destination, they were furious. This town was nothing like the one the priest had described. Instead of a shining city, they found simple houses made of stone and adobe (a mixture of baked clay and straw), belonging to the local Zuni people. Where was the gold? It soon became clear that there had never been any. And so ends the tale—a story of a disastrous treasure hunt that cost many not only their fortunes, but also their lives.

AZTLÁN: LEGENDARY HOMELAND OF THE AZTEC PEOPLE

Six hundred years ago in Mexico, the Aztec people ruled over a large empire. The Aztecs were a tribe of warriors who built their capital city—named Tenochtitlan—in the Valley of Mexico, where Mexico City lies today. But the Aztecs hadn't always lived there. Their legends told of an ancient place somewhere to the north: the original home of the Aztec tribe. This place was called Aztlán.

Searching for Aztlán

If Aztlán was real, where was it? Over the years, experts have suggested several possible locations. Some think that the tiny town of Mexcaltitán in western Mexico is a likely contender. It's built on an island, in a lake, with a street layout similar to Aztec cities. Others believe that Aztlán lay farther to the north, in the southern states of what is now the US.

History and Legend

Historians aren't sure whether Aztlán was an actual location you could pin down on a map, as well as being a symbolic place with an important role in Aztec culture. Many experts believe that the Aztec tribe did move south through Mexico between 1100 and 1300 CE, so perhaps the stories have some basis in events from the past. But it's unlikely there's a lost city of Aztlán hidden somewhere in northern Mexico.

The Place of the Seven Caves

According to the myths, the Aztecs and several other tribes came from a hill with seven caves, each of which housed a different tribe. The story goes that these early people emerged from the caves and settled on an island named Aztlán, in the middle of a lake. The island was home to many beautiful birds, and the waters teemed with fish, so the people never went hungry. But one day, about a thousand years ago, the Aztec people offended their god by cutting down a forbidden tree. And so they were forced to leave their beautiful Aztlán, wandering for many years until they found a new homeland, hundreds of miles to the south.

In some versions of the story, once the Aztecs left Aztlán, thick brambles grew up and covered the city, so the people could never return.

The word "Aztlán" is thought to mean "place of the heron," and the word "Aztec" means "people from Aztlán."

Kantia: Phantom Caribbean island spotted by a German sailor in 1884 but never seen again
Port Royal: Sunken pirate haven (Jamaica)
Ciudad Blanca: The lost city of the Monkey God (Honduras)
El Dorado: The fabled city of gold
Lost City of Z: British explorer Percy Fawcett disappeared while searching for this legendary ancient site in 1925
Colombia
Ukhu Pacha: According to traditional Andean beliefs, this underground realm of the dead was home to a two-headed dragon
Ecuador
Peru
Paititi: Legendary lost Inca city once thought to be hidden in the rainforests east of the Andes
Sierra De La Plata: Mythical mountain of silver ruled by a "White King," searched for by Spanish adventurers
Chile
Davis Land: Curious island discovered by a pirate named Captain Davis in 1687, but never spotted again
Podesta: Puzzling island reportedly sighted by sailors in 1879; later found not to exist
Argentina
Pepys Island: Non-existent island in the South Atlantic; tales of it may have stemmed from confusion with the Falkland Islands
Lost City of the Caesars: Mythical city of diamonds and gold once thought to lie somewhere in Patagonia
Falkland Islands

Central & South America

Hundreds of years ago, when European invaders reached Central and South America seeking land and treasure, they came across the wealthy Aztec and Inca Empires. Hungry for gold, they pushed farther into the continent's dense rainforest, convinced they would stumble upon lost cities of riches. This map shows the legendary places once sought by treasure-seekers, as well as other lost lands, from vanishing islands to pirate capitals.

EL DORADO: THE FABLED CITY OF GOLD

For some, an empty space on a map is a temptation. It stirs a desire to explore; an urge to fill in the blanks. For many years, the unmapped forests of South America lured adventurers with the promise of discovery and riches. Between the fifteenth and seventeenth centuries, European sailors set out for the Americas. This was an age of conquest: the invaders seized land and killed many people. Their goal was to find treasure, and this lust for wealth created one of the world's most enduring legends: a tale of a lost city of glittering gold. This is the legend of El Dorado.

Birth of a Legend

The myth probably began with a person, not a place. "El Dorado" is Spanish for "The Golden One," and refers to a tribal chief of the Muisca people from Colombia. When a new leader was crowned, an unusual ceremony took place. The chief covered himself in gold-dust, rafted to the middle of a mountaintop lake, then plunged in, while others threw gold trinkets into the water from the shore. When Spanish soldiers arrived in Colombia they were fascinated by stories of this ceremony, and the tale grew and changed as it spread. Eventually, the name "El Dorado" came to refer not just to a gold-covered king, but to a whole city made of gold.

In the 1970s the ruins of an ancient city, Ciudad Perdida, were revealed by archaeologists in Colombia. Its stone terraces, cut into the mountainside, date back more than 1,000 years ... but the streets aren't paved with gold!

Ill-Fated Expeditions

Rumors of El Dorado inspired adventurers to search the Amazon Rainforest for a golden kingdom. The English explorer Sir Walter Raleigh launched two expeditions to chase the legend, one in 1595 and another in 1617. He believed that El Dorado lay in Guyana, and he spent a fortune trying to find it. The 1617 trip ended in catastrophe: Raleigh's son was killed in a battle with the Spanish and—when Raleigh returned empty-handed to England—he was executed on the orders of King James I. Across the centuries, the search for El Dorado has claimed hundreds of lives.

When the Spanish seized the capital of the Inca Empire, Cuzco, in the 1530s, they looted large amounts of treasure. This encouraged them to believe there might be other wealthy cities hidden in the rainforest.

Lake of Gold?

Lake Guatavita, in the Andes Mountains, is the sacred lake at the center of the myth. In 1545 Spanish treasure-seekers tried to drain it using buckets, but after several months they had only managed to lower the level by a few meters. In 1562 a large ditch was cut to empty the water, but disaster struck and the channel collapsed. In 1898 an English company invested thousands in draining the lake to search for gold, but the thick mud at the bottom proved impossible to dredge. Finally, in 1965 the Colombian government banned further searches, and the area is now a nature reserve.

CIUDAD BLANCA: THE LOST CITY OF THE MONKEY GOD

The White City, or "Ciudad Blanca" in Spanish—also known as the City of the Monkey God—is a legendary place once thought to lie deep in the jungles of eastern Honduras. This is a region of dense rainforest and overgrown swampland known as the Mosquito Coast. In the twentieth century rumors began to fly that somewhere in the forest was an ancient lost city built from gleaming white stone. Several expeditions set out to search for it. As is often the case with these legends, the City of the Monkey God probably never really existed ... but the remains of other ancient settlements have been discovered in the area.

Locating the Legend

A Legend is Born

The roots of the legend lie in the myths of the local Pech and Tawahka people, who for many years told stories about a sacred, secret place called the "White House." When the Spanish arrived in Honduras in the sixteenth century, their leader Hernán Cortés wrote a letter to the Spanish emperor that mentioned tales of wealthy cities in the region. Over the centuries travelers reported seeing glimpses of a white city from afar, across the jungle. But it wasn't until the twentieth century that the legend picked up steam, and the name "Ciudad Blanca" was born. In the 1930s various expeditions departed from the USA to search for it.

A Tall Tale

In 1939, after a trek into the eastern Honduran rainforest, the US explorer Theodore Morde said he had found the lost city. He described the remains of a defensive wall enclosing several earthen mounds, which he claimed contained buildings. At the center of the city was an overgrown mound which—according to Morde—if excavated, would reveal a temple with a large statue of a monkey god. But many years later, after Morde's death, his journals showed that the entire tale was invented. He hadn't found an ancient city at all, but had made the whole thing up!

In the past, travelers claimed to have seen the white walls of a city in the rainforest. But could these in fact have been limestone cliffs glimpsed from across the jungle?

Lost No Longer?

In 2012 a team of scientists flew over the rainforest and used laser-mapping equipment to scan the ground for buried buildings. They revealed evidence of two settlements, which they believed dated from a thousand years ago. In 2015 they set out to investigate and found an earthen pyramid and a collection of buried carvings of vultures, snakes, and jaguars. Great excitement ensued, and some claimed that the long-lost city had been found. Other archaeologists say there was never one single White City, but instead there are many historic settlements in this area. Intriguing as the story is, there was probably never a huge, ancient monkey-god statue, nor a White City where he was worshipped.

In west Honduras, at the ruins of the Maya city of Copán, there are ancient statues of howler monkey gods. Perhaps that's why people imagined finding monkey statues here, too?

PORT ROYAL: SUNKEN PIRATE HAVEN

Port Royal in Jamaica was once a thriving city, where merchants and traders rubbed shoulders with pirates. Here, seafaring scoundrels would come ashore to spend their ill-gotten gains in the busy dockside taverns. The place was so famous for its marauding visitors that it became known as the "wickedest city on Earth." Even the governor, Henry Morgan, had once been a pirate! But the party didn't last. On the morning of June 7th, 1692, Port Royal was struck by a catastrophic earthquake. At least 2,000 people were killed, and hundreds of buildings were dragged beneath the waves.

Pirate Port

For centuries the Taíno people lived in Jamaica, and the land where Port Royal would one day stand was a fishing village. The Spanish settled here in the 1500s, then the English invaded in 1655. This quiet village became a bustling harbor. It lay on an important shipping route, at the center of the brutal slave and sugar trade. Money flowed in, and Port Royal was soon the wealthiest city in the Caribbean. It was a safe haven for British pirates, who roamed the seas attacking Spanish treasure ships. Piracy was against the law, but the authorities here welcomed pirates' gold, so they usually turned a blind eye to their misdeeds.

Sailors and merchants crowded Port Royal's busy taverns and markets, where stolen goods and precious objects quickly changed hands.

Earthquake!

This notorious city had been built quickly—too quickly. It stood on a spit of sand with flimsy foundations, so when the earthquake hit, the buildings didn't stand a chance. Witnesses talked of the ground splitting open, swallowing people and houses. A series of huge waves followed, rolling in and dumping ships on top of buildings, then sucking everything out to sea. Within minutes, thousands were dead and two-thirds of the city's landmass had been swallowed by the ocean. The remaining people tried to rebuild their town, but disaster struck again in 1703 when a fire tore through the crowded streets. The survivors fled to the mainland and built a new city—Kingston—on the other side of the harbor.

The Welshman Henry Morgan became governor of Jamaica in 1675. He had once been an infamous pirate, attacking Spanish ships and towns across the Caribbean.

At the time of the earthquake, many saw the destruction of Port Royal as a punishment from God for the wickedness of its citizens.

Sunken City

Today, the ruins of this pirates' paradise lie beneath the waters of Kingston Harbor. Parts have been explored by underwater archaeologists. They have salvaged many treasures, including pewter plates, tankards, a chest of silver coins, and even a battered pocket watch whose hands were stopped at 11:43—a ghostly record of the moment the earthquake hit. But the work is slow and difficult: having lain underwater for more than 300 years, the objects are encrusted with rust and coral. Much of the sunken city remains unexplored. Who knows ... perhaps the grave of pirate chief Henry Morgan himself will one day be discovered?

Rica de Oro and Rica de Plata: Legendary islands of gold and silver fruitlessly searched for by Spanish explorers in the 1600s and 1700s
Nan Madol: Ruins of an ancient city built across several islands connected by canals; myths say it was made by twin brothers levitating huge stones
Kibu: Isle of ghosts from the traditional beliefs of some Torres Strait Islanders
Teonimanu: One of the Solomon Islands that sank long ago after an earthquake
Lost City: A few places in northern Australia earn this name because their jutting pillars of rock look like ancient towers
Papua New Guinea
Baralku: Island of the dead
Mount Olga: Once the home of the snake king Wonambi, according to the Dreaming stories of Aboriginal Australians
Australia
Indian Ocean
Sandy Island: Small island shown on maps for more than 100 years, until a research ship in 2012 found it didn't exist
Kangaroo Island: Aboriginal Australian myths remember when this island was connected to the mainland 10,000 years ago
Ancient Aboriginal Homelands: The now-lost homes of Tasmania's Aboriginal Australians once stood in this area; ancient rock art has been found too

HAWAII (USA)

TUANAKI: Mysterious island on which a sailor claimed to have stayed for six days in the 1840s, but which later couldn't be found

HAWAIKI: Homeland of the Māori people

ONASEUSE: Doubtful island described by a sea captain in 1823 but never found again; probably made up

PACIFIC OCEAN

KAIMANAWA WALL: Ancient stones that look human-made, but are in fact a volcanic rock formation

NEW ZEALAND

LAND BRIDGE: New Zealand's North and South Islands were once connected by a land bridge that flooded when sea levels rose 12,000 years ago

AUSTRALASIA & OCEANIA

Aboriginal Australians and Torres Strait Islanders first arrived in this region tens of thousands of years ago. Since then, they have passed down a rich tradition of stories, some of which tell of lands being swallowed by the sea, or mysterious islands of the dead. As well as these legendary places, Oceania is home to thousands of islands, which navigators from the past struggled to keep track of. It's no surprise, then, that mistakes were made, and many islands were "discovered," later to be "undiscovered" when it turned out they didn't exist!

BARALKU: ISLAND OF THE DEAD

The Yolngu people have lived in Arnhem Land in Australia's Northern Territory for a very long time—perhaps 50,000 years. According to Yolngu beliefs, when somebody dies their spirit travels across the sea to the island of the dead, called Baralku. Baralku isn't really somewhere that can be found on a map—it is said to lie far to the east, beyond the sunrise, or sometimes even among the stars.

Venus orbits close to the sun, which means it appears never to rise too high in the sky. This ties in with Yolngu beliefs that Venus is anchored to the island of Baralku by a rope of light.

The planet Venus is one of the brightest stars in the night sky. It's called the Morning Star because it is often visible just before dawn.

Following the Stars

To reach the island of Baralku the spirits of the dead travel in a sacred canoe. They are guided by the Morning Star, Venus, known as Banumbirr to the Yolngu people. Just before dawn, Banumbirr shines in the eastern sky to guide these souls on their journey. When they arrive at the island of the dead, the new souls are greeted by the spirits of their lost friends and relations. Some say that if you look up into the sky at night you may see the campfires of those who have gone before, twinkling along the edges of the Milky Way.

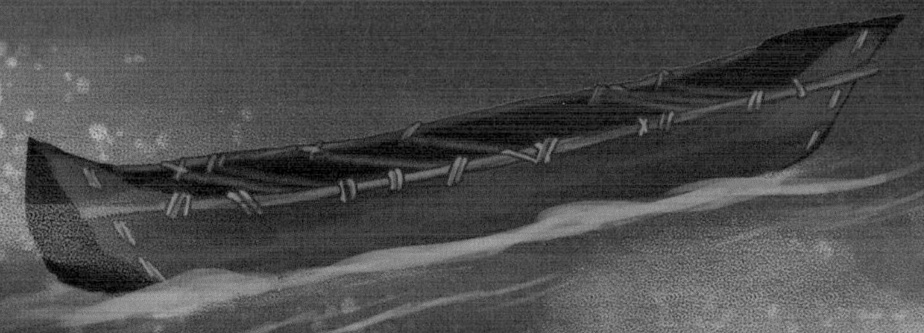

On some nights of the year, certain Yolngu groups hold a Morning Star Ceremony, where they communicate with their ancestors on the Island of the Dead.

Aboriginal Australian people have been called the world's first astronomers, as they have been studying the stars and planets for many thousands of years.

Some believe that if you see a shooting star, it might be a sacred canoe returning to Earth after a journey to Baralku.

A Great Journey

Aboriginal Australians and Torres Strait Islanders have many different creation legends, known as Dreaming or Dreamtime stories. Yolngu mythology says that long ago in the Dreaming, the Morning Star Banumbirr lived on the island of Baralku. She left the island to guide three siblings, the Djanggawul, as they paddled in their canoe to the coast of Arnhem Land. The Djanggawul were powerful creators. They walked across the new landscape, following the rain clouds. When they touched the ground with their digging sticks they created water, animals, and trees, and they later gave birth to the world's first people. This legend has been passed down through the generations, across thousands of years, in stories and songs.

Searching for Baralku

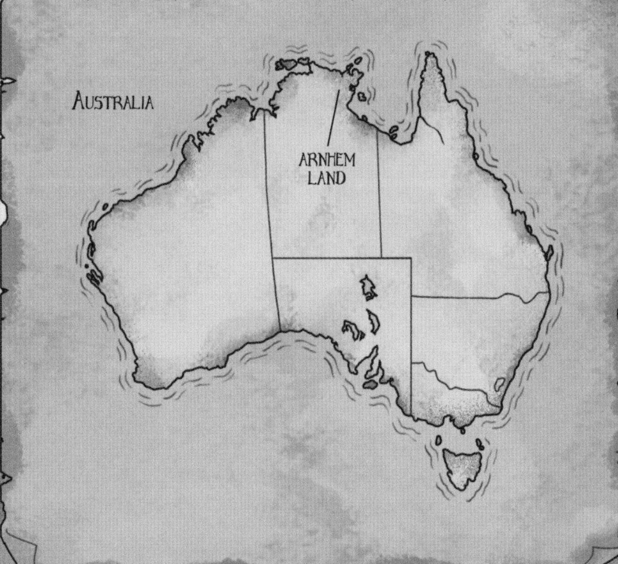

The Māori were the first people to set foot in New Zealand. Some historians believe that they arrived about 800 years ago, traveling in canoes from smaller Polynesian islands to the northeast: perhaps the Cook Islands or the Society Islands. But in the rich mythology of the Māori people, in songs and stories, their original homeland is Hawaiki: an island that lies over the horizon. Is Hawaiki a real place, or an imagined, mythical land? The answer isn't easy, for Hawaiki doesn't fit neatly into a single category.

There are many similarities between Māori language and culture and those of other Polynesian islands, including the Cook Islands, Tahiti, and Hawaii. But despite their similar names, Hawaiki shouldn't be confused with Hawaii.

The Voyage of Kupe

In a famous story from Māori mythology, New Zealand was discovered by a fisherman named Kupe. He found it quite by accident, as a result of chasing an enormous octopus across the ocean. After seeing off the vicious octopus, Kupe returned to Hawaiki, where he told the people about his discovery. Then, a fleet of canoes set sail for New Zealand, or—to give it its Māori name—Aotearoa, which means the "long white cloud." In some versions of the legend Kupe discovered one single landmass, then cut a channel down the middle to create New Zealand's North and South Islands.

The explorer and fisherman Kupe traveled across the Pacific Ocean in his waka hourua (a double-hulled voyaging canoe).

The Beginning and the End

The Māori belief that their ancestors arrived in canoes from the northeast is based on historical events. But over time, this memory of a faraway homeland transformed into a legend. In some myths, Hawaiki is the home of the gods and the site where humans were created. It's the place where life comes from, and where life ends. In Māori mythology, when somebody dies, their soul travels to the tip of New Zealand's North Island, to a place called Te Rerenga Wairua (Cape Reinga). Here, the spirit dives into the ocean and swims to the underworld, which is Hawaiki. In the Māori tradition Hawaiki is both real and mythical; it is the beginning, and the end.

LOST CONTINENTS

Since the days of ancient Greece, when stories were first told about the sunken kingdom of Atlantis, people have imagined cities, islands, or even whole continents that have been swallowed by the ocean. The "lost" continents of Mu and Lemuria are not real places—but Zealandia is an actual continent that sank beneath the waves millions of years ago.

Mu

In the 1870s an archaeologist named Augustus Le Plongeon studied the ruined Maya pyramids of Mexico, and came up with an unusual idea. He declared that the Maya people were originally from a continent called Mu, which sank into the Atlantic. Then, the people of Mu spread out—some to Central America and some to Egypt. According to Le Plongeon, the Egyptian civilization was founded by Queen Moo of the Land of Mu! The idea was intriguing, because it seemed to explain why different societies around the world had similar myths, buildings, and symbols. But there is no scientific evidence for the lost continent of Mu. While the world's landmasses have split up and shifted over millions of years, it's highly unlikely that a huge continent could vanish without a trace.

Kumari Kandam

In myths from south India and Sri Lanka, the ancestors of the Tamil people came from a southern land named Kumari Kandam, which was submerged by a great flood. This story has been around for many hundreds of years, but in the 19th century it became interwoven with tales of the lost continent of Lemuria.

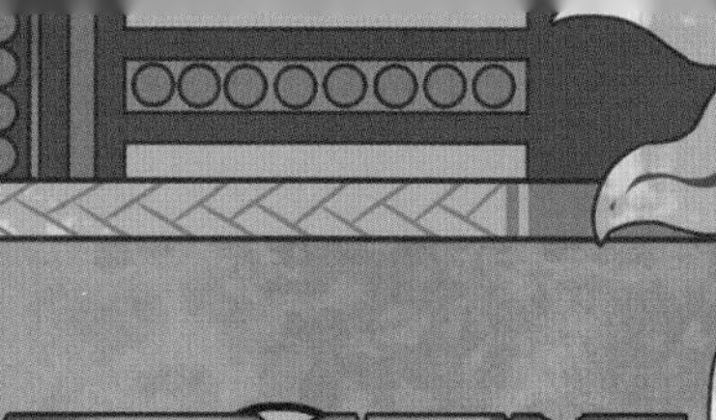

Lemuria

In 1864 a British zoologist called Philip Sclater was puzzled by the fact there were lemur fossils in Madagascar *and* thousands of miles away in India. He mused that perhaps there was once a continent stretching across the Indian Ocean. In honor of the creatures he thought once roamed this now-sunken landmass, he named the continent "Lemuria." Some 19th-century occultists (believers in the supernatural) latched onto the idea. They suggested that survivors from this lost continent, the Lemurians, still live secretly among us. They have four arms, they lay eggs ... and they have superpowers! Nowadays, scientists dismiss the idea of Lemuria. The theory of plate tectonics (see "Shifting Continents") explains the lemur fossils. Madagascar and India were once connected, and split apart more than 80 million years ago, but they were never joined by a lost continent.

Shifting Continents

The Earth's crust is made up of giant pieces called tectonic plates. Beneath them is a layer of semi-molten rock, which slowly swirls around, shifting the plates on top. Over millions of years, the Earth's continents have moved and broken up.

The world 250 million years ago

The world 200 million years ago

The world today

Zealandia

This one is real! Zealandia, known by some as the "eighth continent," is a flooded continent in the Pacific Ocean. It formed about 100 million years ago when a huge piece of land broke off from the ancient supercontinent of Gondwana. Zealandia was once home to dinosaurs and other prehistoric animals, but by 25 million years ago most of it had disappeared underwater. Today, New Zealand and some smaller Pacific islands are the only parts of Zealandia that emerge above the waves.

AGARTHA: IMAGINED KINGDOM INSIDE THE EARTH

For thousands of years people have told stories about the underworld: a hidden place below the ground. Just as travelers once imagined fantastical lands across the ocean or in unexplored parts of the jungle, people have dreamed up extraordinary ideas about what might lie beneath our feet. Over the years, some have suggested that the inside of the Earth was a hollow cavern populated by wise giants, woolly mammoths ... or even aliens! These ideas have been disproved by scientists, but they still crop up in science-fiction stories.

The Hollow Earth?

In the seventeenth century the astronomer Edmond Halley came up with the theory that the Earth might not be solid. His work on magnetic fields led him to suspect that the planet contained several globes stacked inside each other, spinning in different directions. However, in the 1770s scientists proved Halley's idea to be wrong. Over the years several other people suggested that the Earth was hollow, and had its own interior sun. There is no evidence for this theory.

Symmes Holes

In 1818 a US army officer named John Symmes published a letter declaring that the Earth was hollow. He believed each of the poles had a huge opening to another world, inside our own. Although most scientists scorned his ideas, Symmes did win some people over. In 1838 an expedition set off to explore Antarctica, but found no "Symmes Holes" leading to a subterranean world. Aircraft flying over the poles in the early twentieth century found no trace of these holes either, putting paid to Symmes' theory.

When a frozen mammoth was discovered in Siberia in 1846, some claimed it had escaped from inside the Earth, where mammoths were supposedly not extinct.

Agartha

The idea of a hollow Earth led some to imagine entire underground cities. In the 1880s a French writer named Alexandre Saint-Yves described the kingdom of Agartha, which he said lay under the Himalayas. He claimed this land was inhabited by wise beings called the Agarthi, who guarded libraries of ancient knowledge. He suggested that Agartha was linked to other continents through a vast network of underground tunnels, whose locations were known only to those with secret, magical knowledge.

What's Really Inside the Earth?

Of course, none of these far-fetched ideas has any basis in reality. By studying seismic waves from earthquakes, scientists have shown that the Earth has a rocky crust, beneath which is a semi-molten mantle, a liquid outer core, and a dense, solid inner core. It's not really hollow, and there's no inner sun, let alone cities full of wise aliens—or woolly mammoths!

INDEX